D0867978

AT THE HEART OF MONTESSORI

4

THE PRE-SCHOOL CHILD
(3-6 YEARS)

by

CLARE HEALY WALLS

Copyright © 2008 Clare Healy Walls

Cover image courtesy of Kerry Acheson

Waterpark Books ©

All rights reserved. No part of this publication may be
reproduced in any form or by any means – graphic, electronic
or mechanical, including photocopying, recording or
information storage and retrieval systems – without the prior
written permission of the author.

ISBN-10: 0955716853
ISBN-13: 978-0-9557168-5-0 (Waterpark Books)

For Dei

CONTENTS

PART 2: MONTESSORI IN ACTION FOR THE PRE-SCHOOL CHILD

ACKNOWLEDGEMENTS

Thank you to the many people who inspired me as I learned about the Montessori philosophy over a period of 35 years. I want to pay tribute to the Montessori trainers who taught me the basics, with a special word of appreciation for Mrs. Síghle Fitzgerald, who inspired and still inspires me and many others worldwide, together with Mrs. Connie Fahey who left this world a better place for Montessori students and children. The work of Maria Montessori herself continues to re-inspire me every year but my understanding came through much exploring, day and night, at work and at wonderful parties, with colleagues who have become lifelong friends in Oslo, Gothenburg and Cork. Montessori is a practical science therefore I owe a great deal to the Montessori teachers, trainee teachers and children that I have worked with, in many places, over the years, not least my own loving children who allowed me to learn as they grew. Lastly thank you to Kerry who portrayed the simple yet profound essence of Montessori's work in her creative book cover image.

ABOUT THE AUTHOR

Clare Healy Walls lives in Ireland. She established Waterpark Montessori teacher training college, which is based in Oslo and has managed this for twenty years. She is a founding member of Montessori Europe. Clare has an MA in Education Management, holds Montessori St. Nicholas teaching diplomas for pre-school and school and has been involved in the development of Montessori programmes for both Infant/Toddler and Adolescent in Scandinavia. Clare holds a special interest in the application of Montessori principles for all age groups, including adults. In addition to the *At the Heart of Montessori* series, Clare is the author of *The Conscious Parent* and *The Conscious Parent in Action*. She has five children, nine grandchildren and one great-grandchild.

AT THE HEART OF
MONTESSORI
4
THE PRE-SCHOOL CHILD
(3-6 YEARS)

PREFACE

Dr. Maria Montessori

Dr. Maria Montessori was born in Italy in 1870. She grew up under the influence of a traditional father and an ambitious strong-minded mother. She wanted to be an engineer but found being a woman was an obstacle. However she entered univer- sity and qualified as one of the first woman medical doctors in Italy. Her years of study taught her to survive under difficult cir- cumstances. The ethics of the time did not allow for male and female students to work on human bodies at the same time so Maria had to return to the morgue alone at night to do her re- search. When she qualified she worked for some time caring for the poor in Rome. She was always interested in children, their health and the living conditions which affected health. Around this time she was also involved in the emerging movement for women's rights.

Dr. Montessori had a son but the social structure at the time did not allow her to keep him with her as she was unmarried. He was fostered by a family in the countryside and visited by his mother regularly. Dr. Montessori got a job working with children who were mentally deficient. With her keen observa- tional powers and her ever curious mind, she became interested in their education as well as their health. She studied the works of Itard and Séguin, who in turn were influenced by Rousseau and Froebel. In order to understand these works fully she spent many long nights translating them from French into Italian. She was inspired to research further. She adapted and devised sever al educational materials which she used with great success with the children under her care. When they passed examinations, Dr.

Montessori asked herself why the children in the regular schools could not reach much higher levels with good educa-tional stimulation.

On 6th January 1907 Dr. Montessori opened her first Casa de Bambini (Children's House) in Rome. The owners of a large building were concerned about the small children running wild so they invited Dr. Montessori to carry out an experiment with a day nursery for children in pre-school years. She set up a simple room and into this she placed the educational materials which she had devised or adapted from other educators. She employed the caretaker's daughter to take care of the children and in-structed her not to teach them anything, but rather to allow them to use the materials. She observed the children for long periods and added or took away materials according to how the children were attracted to them. The children were shown how to use the materials and, as long as they did not abuse them, were free to use them when they wished.

Within months wonderful things were happening. Children were writing their names, talking about mathematical shapes, behaving very politely and Montessori realised she was making exciting discoveries. People heard about Casa de Bambini and came to see the children. In a world where children were consid-ered noisy and troublesome, these productive well-behaved little people were seen as a miracle. A second nursery was opened by Dr. Montessori the following year. Within a short time she was well known throughout most countries in Europe. In 1911 she published her first of many books, "The Montessori Method". In 1913 she was invited to the USA where she travelled widely, taking her now fifteen year old son, Mario, with her. There she was welcomed enthusiastically and she set up many 'Montes-sori' classrooms.

In the meantime she started the training of teachers to carry on her method but at all times she was reluctant to allow this training to pass out of her personal control. She believed that her method was not easy to use correctly because it involved a basic shift in attitude towards children. Her observations were continually leading her to adapt and develop new materials. She started to work on the method for older children (6-12 years) as far back as 1912 but believed that it was too big a task for one person. With the help of various interested people, the 'Advanced Montessori Method' was developed over a period of many years. Dr. Montessori was also interested in the next level (12-18 years) but she did not have time in her busy life to explore it fully, writing only two chapters to explain her ideas. However it has been developed since her death, and in the early years of the twenty-first century the Montessori method for adolescents is beginning to grow into a thriving movement.

In the latter part of her life, Dr. Montessori's focus went back to the infant and she further developed her ideas on the first years of life. She published "The Absorbent Mind", the book many consider to be her best, in 1949, just a few years before her death, in 1952. Montessori started in Italy, worked for some years in Spain and spent all of World War II in India. She finally settled in Holland and there, with the help of her son Mario, his wife and many devoted friends, set up a centre for developing the Montessori method.

"Her [Maria Montessori's] ideas were formulated after she had laboriously observed the needs of the individual child. Her goal was to develop the whole personality of the child, and her system is based on her strong belief in the spontaneous working of the human intellect. Her three primary principles are observation, individual liberty, and preparation of the environment." (Hainstock, E., 1986)

INTRODUCTION

Clare Healy Walls' infectious enthusiasm for life and keen interest in the welfare of children has encouraged her to share her expertise with others who may be struggling with the noble task of parenthood in the Twenty-first Century. Clare's accumulated wealth of knowledge in this field comes from her own experience as a parent and grand-par-ent as well as her ongoing studies as a teacher and lecturer in the philosophy and pedagogy of Dr. Maria Montessori.

In my opinion, Clare is eminently qualified to share her experiences in the field of Montessori education with those who may find the language in text books written in the early Twentieth Century somewhat difficult to understand. Her special style of 'writing as she talks' makes the content of this set of books more attractive to readers. I am happy to recommend these books as a key to a deeper understand-ing of Montessori's sound philosophy regarding the rearing of children.

Core Principles

Core Principles, the title of the first book in a series of six, and Core Principles in Action, the second book, cover a broad spectrum of Montessori's philosophy of education and its implementation. They envelope the principles of this philosophy, in an attractive and digestible way.

This makes it an easy introduction for the rearing of children and an invaluable reference source for students as well as a refresher for Montessori Educators.

The Infant Toddler Group

Book 3 deals with the characteristics of the child in the period 0-3 years. This is the stage of development when the child is absorbing all that is happening in the environment into the subconscious mind. It covers the period from the pre-natal stage to the third year of life. This is where the foundations are set for all future development.

The Pre-School Child

Book 4 deals with the child of 3-6 years. Montessori considered that the child in this age group should be spending some time at home and some time at pre-school. This pat-tern ensures an easy transition when the child is achieving a certain degree of independence and freedom essential for the building of the personality.

The Elementary School Child

Book 5 relates to the 6-12 years old child and this is considered to be the prime learning stage. Montessori asks us to look at this period of development in two stages i.e. 6-9 and 9-12 years. This is where the abstract mind is taking over from the absorbent mind of the previous stage. Moral development is the hallmark of this age group.

The Adolescent

Book 6 concerns the quality of the personality and ability of the adolescent which reflects the development that has taken place in the previous years. A strong sense of justice is evident and the great power of the imagination, based on reality, is able to cope with the exigencies of life. Finally, we reach the stage that calls for great sensitivity and kind-ness in order to build up the dignity of the human person. Montessori advocated a special environment for the adoles-cent and young adult. She called it 'Erdkinder,' a school of experience in the elements of social life.

"In order to understand the child so as to be able to edu-cate him, we must know life in its entirety" (Montessori, M., unpublished lecture, London 1937) Montessori looked to the child for guidance in preparing a philosophy of education that would embrace the develop-ment of the person from childhood to adolescence.

Síghle P. Fitzgerald, August 2008

AUTHOR'S NOTE

The *At the Heart of Montessori* series of books is based on lectures I presented over a number of years. The style is therefore informal and the reader will notice occasional inconsistencies and apparent errors in language structure or punctuation. We ask for the reader's understanding and hope this will not interfere with your enjoyment or learning. An unconventional referencing system is used in many places to facilitate readers in identifying the source of the quotation. There are a large number of editions of the same books by Dr. Montessori, some of them published the same year and often using varying chapter numbers.

AT THE HEART OF MONTESSORI

At the Heart of Montessori 1 & 2 will help the reader to understand the core Montessori principles and how they are applied generally. In order to understand any of the other four books relating to children of different age groups, 1 & 2 should be read first.

PART 1:

MONTESSORI
&
DEVELOPMENT OF
THE PRE-SCHOOL CHILD

1.

CHILD DEVELOPMENT 3-

6 YEARS

> The Absorbent Mind is the driving force in the child 0-6 years. In the first three years the child unconsciously absorbed the world. Between 3 and 6 years the child takes what he has absorbed and works to make it conscious.

1.1. Looking Back - the Child 0-3 Years

In the first three years of life the child is mostly unconscious, using the absorbent mind to create the basics of a personality and to learn the basic skills of life. This is also referred to as the pre-conscious stage. The 'spiritual embryo' (or 'psychic embryo') is the name given to that period by Dr. Montessori, referring to the fact that the developing spirit or psyche is very sensitive yet protected in a special way. It is creating the basic functions according to an inbuilt plan ('nebulae') and to do this, it takes from the environment what it needs.

In these years we can see that the child needs much attention and care. He absorbs his environment and creates a range of skills and a personality from this. Yet we cannot force him to do things. The pre-conscious urge ('horme') drives him to acquire certain experiences according to his sensitive periods. He takes what he needs from us and from the environment but uses it in his own way. Every experience is stored in the pre-conscious memory ('mneme') and from this is built the man of the future. Physically the child grows rapidly from a helpless infant to an upright toddler very fast. During this time he has to learn to control every aspect of this new body. Mentally he starts as an infant with no knowledge of how to cope in the world and within three years has full use of a language and knows about all the basic things in his environment. Emotionally the first three years is a time of great change but basic emotional skills in relating to people closely are learned in these years. The nature of the unconscious absorbent mind protects these sensitive emotions to some extent and allows the child to learn from his experiences, whether they are good or bad. Socially the child develops in three years, starting as an uncommunicative infant and by 3 years he is a charming active member of his social group.

1.2. Characteristics 3-6 years

At about 2 - 2.5 years the child starts to become conscious. By 3 years of age all children have started the process of making conscious what was unconscious. The vast amount of information taken in the first three years is now slowly brought to consciousness through activity. This happens against a background of a very active life, where the child moves about her environment refining her knowledge and skills. Broadly speaking we can say that the child laid down all the basics of a personality in the first three years and will now refine this to a stage where it can be used in society. By the time a child comes out of this period, when he is 6 years of age, he is capable of living in the world alone. Our society is rather too sophisticated for this to happen but if we look at the skills of a 6 year old we can see that he could care for herself in a simpler society.

1.3. Overview of Physical Development 3-6

The body of the 3 year old is getting stronger yet he is still soft with a slight babyish look around his face, hands and body. A 3 year old has that appeal of infancy in his sweet and innocent appearance. [Nature has cleverly given that appeal to very young children so that we adults are attracted to them and therefore care for them!] Then over the following three years, he grows taller, bonier, loses his chubbiness and becomes stronger. At 3 years children are susceptible to many illnesses, yet by 6 years they have built up stronger immunities and resist illness. At 3 years he has not long finished growing his first set of teeth, and at about 6 years he will start to grow his permanent teeth. This period is a bridge from infancy to middle childhood, characterised by gradual but obvious moves towards strength and independence.

The child of 3 years is very active physically, capable of running, jumping and climbing. By 6 years he has made these skills more refined, running faster and falling less often. We can see an even greater difference in the use of the hand. The child can do basic tasks with her hand at 3 years, feeding, dressing, carrying and so on. In the next three years he refines this so that he can hold a pencil and write, can use a paintbrush, can sew and can use many utensils. Dr. Montessori saw the development of the hand in these years as being of special significance. She noted that it was closely connected with the refinement of intellectual skills and was a key feature in bringing to consciousness what was absorbed unconsciously in the first three years.

1.4. Overview of Cognitive and Linguistic Development 3-6

Cognitively this period is also a time of refinement. The child has absorbed much information and has laid a foundation within the psyche. It is now necessary to put this into a format which is more orderly and more accessible. The mind is still an absorbent mind but is now working consciously. From 3 to 6, years, the child continues to absorb information but is now trying to relate all information within an orderly mental framework. The sensitive period for order is becoming more mental in its focus and this influences the manner of learning. Because the mind is still absorbent, the child remains in a phase where sensorial experience is important. These factors influence the way in which the child learns and how much he learns. Dr. Montessori believed that there is much learning taking place but it needs to have a sensorial basis. Children can learn to read, write and do mathematics if they are presented in a sensorial way. This concept is the one which first made Dr. Montessori famous. She realised that children of 3-6 years were rather clever, but their mode of understanding and learning is different from that of the adult.

"The period of childhood when a child starts to become conscious of himself and his senses are in a creative state is particularly subject to suggestions" (Montessori, M., The Secret of Childhood, Chapter, The Substitution of the Personality, 1966)

The basics of language were laid in the first two and a half years. From then until 5 or 6 years of age the child refines this significantly. Grammar and clarity of speech become points of interest and fun and the child learns to bring language to a quite sophisticated level by 6 years. Vocabulary increases greatly. The sensitive period for language is active until 6 years.

1.5. Overview of Emotional and Social Development 3-6

The child of 3-6 years is in control of his emotions more than the younger toddler. He is developing a conscious will. No longer is he driven totally by the powerful horme. However the sensitive periods are still in force and a child will become frustrated if he cannot satisfy his inner needs.

The child needs the affection and care of adults but he seeks an increasing level of independence. Time away from his parents is important in this phase. Yet it must be time in a secure setting, providing emotional stability and intellectual challenge.

Socially the child moves out of the totally self-absorbed time of the infant to needing other children to associate with. Many of the activities attractive to a 3-6 year old require the involvement of others. The child is practising his language and his social skills. However the child is as yet not really interested in friendships. Every social encounter is mainly of importance because it reflects what he himself is doing.

2.

MONTESSORI & SOCIAL DEVELOPMENT 3-6

> "The first essential for the child's development is concentration. It lays the whole basis for his character and social behaviour." (Montessori, M., The Absorbent Mind, Chapter, Social Development, 1988)

2.1. Development of a Personality

We can interpret the word personality to mean the manner in which an individual develops inherited human potentials in order to function effectively in this world. The child is born with human potential. Environmental experience and choices determine how this is developed. We all have different personalities and the extent to which this is the result of inherited traits or environmental conditions, is an ongoing debate amongst scientists of different disciplines. Nature versus nurture!

Dr. Montessori also used the word 'character'. Her interpretation of that word meant the strength of a person's will, the ability to control oneself and the ability to function effectively and happily within society. Dr. Montessori believed that character or moral development, emotional development and social development were all closely tied together.

2.2. Social Development 3-6

"The first essential for the child's development is concentration. It lays the whole basis for his character and social behaviour. He must find out how to concentrate, and for this he needs things to concentrate upon." (Montessori, M., The Absorbent Mind, Chapter, Social Development, 1988)

The above quotation sums up the centre of Dr. Montessori's philosophy on social development. She believed that the most important thing to come out of her method was the level of deep concentration which the children reached.

Children working individually have to move about the Montessori classroom, choosing what to do and following their own needs. In this way they learn to concentrate. In order to do that they must co-operate with others, be considerate of others' space, wait for them to finish with something, learn to be aware of others' needs and so on.

"Out of this comes a change, an adaptation, which is nothing if not the birth of social life itself. Society does not rest on personal wishes, but on a combination of activities which have to be harmonised." (Montessori, M., The Absorbent Mind, Chapter, Social Development, 1988)

The point to note that is different in Dr. Montessori's approach to social development from that of many other educationalists, is that she realised that this change, this "birth of social life" cannot take place if each member of the group is not in a position to control herself. Therefore learning to concentrate and to gain self-discipline must be given priority. Social development will follow naturally.

2.3. Social Embryo

The social embryo was a term given by Dr. Montessori to the child 3-6 years. She did not use the term as often as she used 'spiritual embryo' (0-3 years) but it follows the same principles. The child is in an embryonic state for social life during this period 3-6 years. She is still developing her individual personality and uses adults and other children to do this. Individual needs will get priority over group needs for a child of this age. She is not yet a fully participating member of society. However she is developing the skills needed to become a member of society. She is putting much effort into doing that without being aware of the end purpose of it all. She is in embryonic social stage.

The child is learning social graces. She loves to play games about 'good manners'. Grace and courtesy lessons are popular. She loves to imitate adults in playing games based on social customs, for example 'going to work', 'cooking the dinner', 'going shopping', 'talking on the telephone'. From these activities she is learning social customs and skills. In Montessori schools, there are many other practical life activities which the child is attracted to and which prepare for social life, cleaning, washing, laying tables and similar.

At the same time she is building her own individual character and the ability to control herself, by concentrating on activities and practising making choices. Her character is then ready at 6 years to take part in society.

The child is learning to co-operate with others. She does not know that that is what she is learning because her motivation is to follow her own individual needs. But she cannot do that unless she takes the needs of others into account. What better way to learn social co-operation?

Children of this age accept that things are done in a certain way, they do not need long explanations. Their need to adapt and to learn about the world, supported by the sense of order, means that they want to do something because it is done that way by everyone else. Therefore when we say she must wait until somebody is finished with the pink tower before she can use it, she accepts that rule happily. She has seen that when she is using something it will not be taken from her before she is ready. She does not need to become possessive about things, she realises that she can use them when and for as long as she needs to. The importance of this learning led Dr. Montessori to insist that there was only one of each exercise in a Montessori classroom.

2.4. Society by Cohesion

Montessori classrooms have several rules which are absolutely essential to the proper functioning of the method. The reasons behind these rules are to a large extent based on the principles stated above. Examples of these rules are:

- Only one piece of each material

- A child may use an exercise as long as she needs to, others must wait. There is no such thing as 'turns' in a Montessori class.

- One may not interrupt someone who is working, that also leads to the talking quietly all the time rule.

- One must always walk around a mat or work area, never across it.

- Exercises must be put back in their right place before another child takes it to use it. (The putting back is part of the exercise.)

- Children must not interrupt the teacher when he is talking to another child. There should be a code for attracting teacher's attention and then waiting.

Inexperienced teachers may not give enough attention to the above rules and often find that the class is not working as it says in the books. The social rules of a class are very important and much time should be given to them at the beginning of the year. When children are functioning naturally in the Montessori social environment, they develop a bonding with the group. It is not a social group in the way older children or adults make groups. However they do care about each other in a special way. They have a 'society by cohesion'. They are 'cohesed' or glued together without being involved in each other's development. Each is concentrating on her own development but cares what happens to others simply because what happens in the world is interesting. At the same time they are starting to learn to empathise with others and their feelings. This is the basis for later organised social life.

> *"This warp corresponds to social cohesion. Preparation for human society is based on the activities of children who act, urged on by the needs of their nature, in a limited world corresponding to the frame [of the weaver]. They end by becoming associated, all with the same end in view [...]. Society does not depend entirely on organisation, but also on cohesion, and of these two the second is basic and serves as foundation for the first." (Montessori, M., The Absorbent Mind, Chapter, Cohesion in the Social Unit, 1988)*

2.5. Age Range

An essential feature of the Montessori environment is the fact that age groups are mixed. In the first place, Dr. Montessori pointed out that children of the same age make a very boring un-stimulating group. There are many other benefits to this system and overall it makes a more natural social setting within which to learn social norms. Let us examine a class with three, four and five year olds in it.

- The three year olds benefit by watching the older children. They subconsciously realise that they will come to that stage soon. They look to the older children for guidance and advice. In many instances they get actual lessons from the older children. The bond between two children is closer than between teacher and child. This works academically and socially.

- The four year old is in the middle. It is a time of consolidation. She still has older children as models but can start to be a model for the younger ones.

- The five year old is given the opportunity to see how much she has learned when she works beside the younger children. Yet she does not have to feel superior about this. She realises that we each must go through different stages. She is attracted to the younger children and wants to help. In this helping she gets practice in what she has learned himself. She reinforces what she has learned, allowing it to become fixed before she moves on to the next age group. This too applies academically and socially.

2.6. Normalisation & Deviations

Character development is based on learning to concentrate and then gaining self-discipline. Dr. Montessori strongly asserted that the natural nature of human children is towards good. She states that "[...] it is natural for man to feel this urge to go forward" and then that "This adaptation to the world about one occurs in the first six years. Here then are to be found the origins of character" [See also Dr. Montessori's diagram on Circles of Attraction for Social Types] (Montessori, M., The Absorbent Mind, Chapter, Character Building, 1988)

Dr. Montessori observed that children's misbehaviours were in fact deviations from the norm. Deviations in children 3-6 years were the result of diverted energies in the first three years of life. The horme pushed the child to behave in one way and this was often blocked. The energy was diverted and became misbehaviour. This misbehaviour she called a deviation. In *The Secret of Childhood*, Montessori gives an account of what she means by deviations. She discusses in detail the various forms which deviations take. She broadly grouped them into three types:

- The quiet passive child

- The noisy boisterous child

- The over-imaginative child

She was anxious to point out that the first and last of these are often seen as normal. However, if closely observed we see that the child has simply escaped from her true nature by adopting conformist or attractive behaviour. Dr. Montessori then further defines deviations, dividing them into fugues, barriers, attachment, possessiveness, desire for power, inferiority complex, fear and lies. She argues that each is caused by a deviation of energy, a restriction to the horme. Some are easier to cure than others. But the cure for each is the same. (Montessori, M., The Secret of Childhood, 1966)

Dr. Montessori went on to show us, how, through purposeful activity, a child could concentrate deeply, how deviations disappeared and a new child appeared. This process she called 'normalisation'. She said this was the normal state for the child. She did not intend that all children would be the same. Rather, she believed that, by nature, children act spontaneously and happily, that they like work and are kind to others.

> *"Such deviations cannot be attributed to the personality itself. They come from a failure to organise the personality. [...] but when the attractions of the new environment exert their spell, offering motives for constructive activity, then all these energies combine and the deviations can be*

dispersed. A unique type of child appears, a 'new child'; but really it is the child's true 'personality' allowed to construct itself normally." (Montessori, M., The Absorbent Mind, Chapter - The Child's Contribution, 1988)

See also Dr. Montessori's diagram on Normal and Deviated Character Traits in Children in the same chapter in *The Absorbent Mind*. The importance of this process of normalisation cannot be underestimated. Dr. Montessori herself said it was:

"the most important single result of our whole work." (Montessori, M., The Absorbent Mind, Chapter, The Child's Contribution, 1988)

The process is based on creating opportunities for concentration, a very special deep kind of concentration. "The essential thing is for the task to arouse such an interest that it engages the child's whole personality [...] one is tempted to say that the children are performing spiritual exercises, having found the path to self-perfectionment and of ascent to the inner heights of the soul." (Montessori, M., The Absorbent Mind, Chapter, The Child's Contribution, 1988)

To allow this to happen we need to provide work and freedom. Purposeful activities and the freedom to choose them are essential to the process of normalisation. If this is the most important result of a Montessori class we must surely give all our priorities to creating such an atmosphere. Learning other things, good behaviour, math, language, creativity, will all follow naturally. However the reverse will not happen, normalisation will not follow other learning. How can we at any time not give priority to providing freedom and purposeful activities? It is a point a Montessori teacher should contemplate every single day.

Within a Montessori class we set up conditions which encourage concentration. One of these conditions is the 'work cycle' (Montessori, M., The Advanced Montessori Method Part 1, 1965). The work cycle is a three hour period which Dr. Montessori said we ought to allow for the children's working period, in order for full concentration to develop.

See Part 2 for more information on Purposeful Activities.

2.7. Will & Obedience

In the old fashioned way teachers believed that obedience came about by 'breaking' the will of the child. But the will needs to be strengthened not broken. It needs to be practised. Just like any other skill it develops through practice. In the first years it is the horme, the unconscious will, which drives the actions of the child. Gradually the conscious will is developed but this takes time and practice. Out of this grows the power of self-discipline.

"Discipline, therefore, is not a fact, but a way, in the course of which the child masters with a precision, which one might call scientific, the idea of goodness. But above all he tastes the supreme pleasures associated with the inward order [...]." (Montessori, M. The Discovery of the Child, Chapter, Discipline in the Children's House, 1966)

Obedience is something which we as adults often connect with the will of the child. Dr. Montessori describes three levels of obedience in two of her books. They are slightly different but follow a similar theme. The development of will and the corresponding ability to obey take place over a period from about 1 year (or earlier) to about 4 years of age.

In *The Discovery of the Child* Montessori talks of three levels of the development of the will and three corresponding levels of obedience.

1. There is a subconscious condition, guided by inward impulse and this cannot be reproduced at will. The child does not and cannot obey

2. A conscious character appears and the will assists its growth. Sometimes the child obeys but cannot always obey because there is no pleasure in obeying if it does not correspond with the inner impulse.

3. The will is able to direct and instigate acts themselves, responding also to external commands. The child is delighted to obey.

(Montessori, M. The Discovery of the Child, Chapter, Discipline in the Children's House, 1966)

In *The Absorbent Mind* she describes three levels of obedience which are slightly advanced on the above but follow the same type of progression.

1. The child can obey but not all the time. This is confusing for adults who need to be aware of the complexity of obedience.

2. The child can obey all the time. His actions "can be directed not only by his own will, but also by the will of another". This is the highest form of obedience which most teachers aspire to.

BUT

3. Obedience becomes an attractive activity in itself. "It is as if the child had become aware that the teacher could do

things beyond his own powers". He wants the teacher to give commands so that he can have the pleasure of carrying them out. Children start to anticipate the commands of the teacher.

(Montessori, M., The Absorbent Mind, 1988)
An example to demonstrate this last stage is the Silence Game, where the children sit in complete silence but in great excitement as they await the teacher calling each name.

2.8. Error

Dr. Montessori was strongly against rewards and punishments. She believed that they were superfluous. She said prizes insulted the free child. She may ask for approval but prizes and unasked for praise distract from the true goal, the joy of the work in itself. Punishments and grading of work were to Dr. Montessori not only useless but quite harmful.

"Only exercise and experience can correct a disability, and it takes long practice to acquire the various kinds of skill that are needed. If you tell a pupil that he lacks the ability to do something [...] this is not a correction. It is a statement of fact [...]. If anything is likely to make the character indecisive it is the inability to control matters without having to seek advice." (Montessori, M., The Absorbent Mind, Chapter, Mistakes and their Correction, 1988)

This issue is the most difficult of the Montessori principles for teachers to accept. In many of our pre-schools we still award 'stars' and other 'treats'. Some adults believe that children need grading, rewards and punishments to progress. Grading is a type of reward or punishment. It attempts to motivate from the outside and not from the inside, where the only long-lasting motivation comes from. "How can a nought (zero) correct anyone's defects?" (Montessori, M., The Absorbent Mind, Chapter, Mistakes and their Correction, 1988)

Teachers find it hard to accept that children can learn without the pressure of adults. "How will she know she is wrong if I do not tell her? How will she make progress if I do not show her where she is going wrong?" But as Dr. Montessori says,

> *"It may happen that the child makes a mistake without knowing it; but also the teacher can err unconsciously [...]. The teacher who sets out with the idea that she is perfect, and never notices her own mistakes, is not a good teacher." (Montessori, M., The Absorbent Mind, Chapter, Social Development, 1988)*

The solution to this problem is twofold. In the first place the teacher must be creative in transferring the teaching and correcting to the environment. In that way the child gets the necessary feedback without adult interference and is self-motivated.

In the second place we must all develop a friendly attitude towards error. Everyone makes mistakes but they have a purpose. We learn from them if we are willing to recognise their worth. Teachers must never be afraid of admitting their mistakes to the children. It creates a good model for the children if teachers are comfortable with error. If a teacher does not know the answer to a question, she can say "Let us go and find out together" or "Let me show you where you can find the answer to that question" or "I will find out about that tomorrow for you."

The control of error is a major part of the Montessori classroom. Where possible, control is built into the material. Children see their own mistakes and take pleasure in correcting them. They learn from this control and learn more than the facts. They learn self-discipline and self-management.

The control of error has another side benefit. It becomes a point of interest in itself. It encourages concentration. As Dr. Montessori pointed out:

"It becomes a link, and is certainly a bond of fellowship between human beings [...]. To detect some small error in a grown-up does not produce lack of respect in the child or loss of dignity in the grown-up. The error becomes impersonal and is then amenable to control. In this way small things lead to great." (Montessori, M., The Absorbent Mind, Chapter, Mistakes and their Correction, 1988)

2.9. The Adult & Social Development 3-6

As with all other aspects of the role of the adult, the main thing an adult must do to support the child socially is to offer guidance and then avoid interference. Dr. Montessori points out that when adults interfere in the budding social life of children they nearly always make mistakes. The example she gives is 'walking on the line', a group of children walking in a circle. One child may be walking in the wrong direction and the teacher may be tempted to turn her around. But the child himself will see her mistake and if not, the other children will soon show her.

The adult will offer the child affection and warmth in her development but will try to stand back and allow independence to develop. Meanwhile the adult has an important role to play in setting up the situation where the child can learn social skills. Opportunities for concentration, a correct age balance in the class, controls in the exercises and many more things are necessary for the child to learn all that we have discussed above. This takes work, training and dedication on the part of the adult. This is not 'teaching' as traditionally know, nor is 'caring' for the children but it is an essential role. Sometimes we fear that we are not enough involved with the children and spend our time working with other things. We have to be deeply convinced of the importance of what we are doing in order to do it effectively. That is how we will help the children to develop to their maximum potential.

3.

SENSITIVE PERIODS 3-6 YEARS

Nature has created special times when the child's energy is focused on constructing particular skills or functions. These times, called 'sensitive periods' are important to the child's development.

3.1. Sensitive Periods 0-6

Hugo de Vries discovered sensitive periods in animals but Dr. Montessori noticed that children also make use of sensitive periods. Sensitive periods support the child in the work he does in order to acquire what is needed to build his personality. A child needs physical, mental and social skills to complete the person he will become. Each of these has to be constructed. Sensitive periods are important tools in that construction.

A sensitive period is a time in a child's life when he is especially sensitive to certain stimuli, and is attracted to certain activities. This period does not last and is connected to acquiring a particular trait or skill. When the sensitive period passes the child will have developed a new skill or function. If the time passes and the child is denied access to whatever his sensitive period is driving him to do, he will not acquire the skill.

"It is a transient disposition and limited to the acquisition of a particular trait. Once this trait, or characteristic, has

22

been acquired, the special sensibility disappears."
(Montessori, M., The Secret of Childhood, Chapter,
Psychic Development, 1966)

3.2. The Function of Sensitive Periods

The child is building the man or woman of the future. The sensitive periods ensure that the child is attracted to the right kind of experiences to allow him to create whatever skill or trait that is due to be created according to an inbuilt programme. Because of that human developmental trait, we notice that young children all over the world tend to develop certain skills at about the same age, regardless of race or background.

"[...] a child's psychic development does not take place by chance [...] [it] does not originate in external stimuli but is guided by transient sensibilities, that is, by temporary instincts intimately connected with the acquisition of specific traits. Although this takes place within an external environment, the environment itself is more of an occasion than a cause; it simply provides the necessary means for spiritual growth. (Montessori, M., The Secret of Childhood, Chapter, Psychic Development, 1966)

Dr. Montessori constantly refers to the fact that we as humans have an inbuilt programme but the way in which we develop that programme is not pre-ordained. Therefore we have the opportunity, as children, to develop according to our own culture. We, as a species, are able to advance rapidly in many technological and cultural ways and yet our children can absorb these new ways as part of their basic personalities. We have only to look at the ease with which young children can use computers and we see evidence of this.

Sensitive periods play a very important part in the development of the child and therefore in the development of the human race. A young child that climbs the stairs, slides down, climbs again, slides down and repeats this about ten times

23

leaves adults amazed because there seems to be no purpose to the activity. The child is in a sensitive period for movement, a particular kind of movement, climbing. Therefore that activity attracts the child deeply *"like a light that shines on some objects but not on others" (Montessori, M., The Secret of Childhood, Chapter, Psychic Development, 1966)*. What is apparently without purpose to an adult has a very important purpose for a child. He is actually building up the skill of climbing. He is building the man of the future.

> *"It is not right to say the mother and father have made their child. Rather we should say: 'The child is the father of the man.' "(Montessori, M., The Secret of Childhood, Chapter. Order, 1966)*

Psychologists and educationalists after Montessori have identified that this type of activity is 'play', the means by which children learn most skills. Montessori preferred to call it 'work', as it is the work of the child to create his personality and his skills. He is working to create the man of the future.

3.3. Recognising Sensitive Periods

Sensitive periods have general titles, for example, the sensitive period for movement, but there are many mini-stages of this, such as a sensitive period for releasing grip or the sensitive period for climbing. The same pattern is observable in the overall sensitive period and in the 'mini-stages'. Adults will be able to recognise sensitive periods in children by observing particular things.

Repetition

Firstly take note of new skills or traits acquired by the child and ask yourself how he learned or is learning this. What has he been practising lately? Has your baby been dropping his spoon from a height day after day until you are tired of picking it up?

He is probably practising releasing his grip and learning about cause and effect. These are two very important things in our lives and therefore they need much practice. Take note of other activities about this time. Maybe he plays transferring a toy from one hand to another. Then you may find that he suddenly loses interest in this activity and starts to focus on something completely different like making noises as he bangs his spoon off his plate. Watch him and see has he learned something new about releasing his grip? Can he transfer objects with greater ease? When he drops something now does he know where it has gone?

A Special Attraction

Secondly take note of the things which seem to especially attract the child just now. Are there certain activities that the child wants to go back to again and again? Are there certain things or situations which particularly interest him? Have you seen a two and a half year old playing with water? He may be obsessed with watching the water run and splash on objects. He may want to do it day after day, again and again. The bathroom will become flooded but he does not notice. He does not feel cold when he gets wet. He is only fascinated with this running water. The adults may scold him, may charm him away and divert him with other activities. But he will come back and try to get at the water again.

Cycle of Activity

In terms of any particular day the child will tire of this activity when his 'cycle of activity' is finished. Suddenly he stops. To adults there is no logic to when this happens. Maybe he has not used all the utensils we provided for him to play with in the water. To us nothing is 'finished'. But an inner 'cycle of activity' is finished. He has had enough for to-day. He has learned as much as possible for one session. Take note of his face. It will usually wear a look of satisfaction. A job well done!

The End of a Sensitive Period

The child will come back to the activity related to the sensitive period day after day for days or weeks or months. Suddenly he does not find it interesting any more. Maybe you have built him a special unit to play with water but it took you a month to build it. You find it is redundant before he gets it. The sensitive period is over. There is nothing we can do about it. It is totally controlled by an inner guide.

In the first three years of life this inner guide seems to be very well protected from adult influence. From three to six years, sensitive periods are less intense and tend to last a little longer. Therefore we get a chance to 'catch up' with them before they are gone. We can observe, note the sensitive period and then provide what is needed.

3.4. Changes within Sensitive Periods

There are stages within a sensitive period. The focus changes at times during the overall sensitive period. The sensitive period for language lasts from birth to 6 years but changes its particular focus over the years. These changes are very closely related to the changes in the development of the child. The development of language will dictate the stages in the sensitive period for language. The development of movement will dictate the stages in the sensitive period for movement. The development of the intellect will dictate the stages of the sensitive period for order. Do not forget that all development is inter-related. Language, movement and order are all developing side by side and are dependent on each other. Nothing develops in isolation.

If you examine the sensitive periods you will find a broad pattern which fits what Dr. Montessori describes in the Stages of Development. (See *At The Heart of Montessori (1) - Core Principles).*

In the first three years of life the basics are laid down and in the next three years they are refined. For example a child gets a deep understanding of order absorbed into his body in the first

26

three years. He spends the next three years refining this and making it more abstract and focussing more on mental order. A child learns all the basic movements (large and fine motor movement) in the first two to three years and spends the next few years refining these. He learned to walk but after 3 years he practises jumping and skipping. He learned to grab and release but later he can use a pencil to write. The child's intense interest in learning new words from two and a half to six years is a refinement of the basic language structure laid down in the first two and a half years. It will not always be possible to find this pattern in every detailed sensitive period but it is a broad guide to explain why sensitive periods change.

In the period 3-6 years the absorbent mind of the child is becoming conscious. We need to see the importance of this process in the development of the sensitive periods. You will note that the sensitive periods 3-6 years are all dealing with refinement and moving towards clearly defined conscious ideas.

3.5. Sensitive Period for Order 3-6

One of the main sources of conflict between toddlers and adults is the sensitive period for order. This leads to many tantrums and in fact the phrase 'the terrible twos' probably arose out of a lack of understanding of the sensitive period for order. The sensitive period for order lasts from 0-6 years.

In the period 3-6 years children are still in a sensitive period for order but now it manifests itself more in intellectual activities. It is not a source of major conflict between adult and child in this phase. The child has absorbed vast amounts of information in the first three years of life and needs to place it in some kind of order in the period 3-6 years.

> "Now, abstract ideas are always limited in number, while the real things we encounter are innumerable. These limited abstractions increase in value with their precision." (Montessori, M., The Absorbent Mind, Chapter, Through Culture and the Imagination, 1988)

27

Dr. Montessori tells us that children need to put the vast number of impressions and ideas received in a kind of filing system so that they are of value to the intellect. In the period 3-6 years, children are trying to make conscious what was unconscious. They try to keep these things in some kind of order so that they can make sense of them. They like to compare things to already established ideas. If you watch small children, you will see that they like to keep things in the same place and follow the same routines each day. They want stories told in the same sequence each time. They even keep their bedrooms tidy for these few years. They get great joy when they learn to understand something new so they do not want it to be changed the next day. As they get older this need is not so strong because they become more and more confident in the way the world works.

Although order in the environment is not as important as it was for the one and two year old, children of 3-6 years thrive on order. They will learn faster and will be more content when they live in an orderly world. Parents need to remember this when they are changing the furniture or the babysitter. This will have a much stronger effect on a four year old than it does on an eight year old, and the strongest impact will be on the child under three years.

3.6. Order and the Prepared Environment 3-6

The Montessori prepared environment for 3-6 years will be orderly in its physical layout and in its routines. Shelves will have exercises neatly laid out with colour coding to help identify where things belong. Everything must be kept in the same place all the time. The adult will ensure that no pieces are missing from exercises and that everything is in good condition. Given that the children are in the sensitive period for order, they will work well within this kind of environment and they will co-operate in keeping it orderly.

Exercises have order within them. They are presented in the same way all the time. Details such as where to put the lid of the box are noted by the children so we must not keep changing. An example of how an exercise can be made in an orderly way is to use pink for mirror polishing, a pink basket with pink polishing cloths and perhaps a pink box for putting the soiled cloths into. Use a blue colour code for silver polishing and so on. The children find it much easier to cope with this kind of structure and they can focus on the exercise without the frustration of looking for missing things.

Routines must also be orderly. They should not be changed too often. If the adult does the weather chart every day at the beginning of circle time, they may be quite disorientated if she forgets and does it at the end of circle time. No doubt some child will remind the adult. The sensitive period will insist on that!

3.7. Culture 3-6

A child absorbs his own culture in the first six years. Sensitive periods help to focus on particular aspects of this so that they can be learned well. By culture we mean all the ways, mannerisms and tastes of the people. If a child in the first six years hears his father playing rock music on his stereo every day, he will absorb a love of rock music. One brother may become a rock music player and another brother may just feel comfortable for the rest of his life whenever he hears this kind of music. It has become a part of these children.

Dr. Montessori refers to the fact that a human being will always be happiest in the land of his birth because he has developed a love of the things he absorbed in his early years. While children absorb most culture simply by being there, we can observe them actively taking in certain things as they observe intently. Children want to help their parents in household chores and in that way they learn the 'local' way of doing things. Montessori 'practical life' exercises are always related to the local culture for this reason. Religious practices are fascinating to children especially from about 4-6 years. They love the ceremony and ritual involved. Many people do not practise religion since they have become adults, but they still love the smells and sounds of the church because they have absorbed it as part of their culture. Another opportunity to observe children actively learning about their culture is to watch a one-year old when he is in the company of a group of people talking to each other. He will watch intently the gestures and movements they make. When he begins talking he will start to make the same gestures. That is why Italians make one kind of gesture and Norwegians make completely different gestures when they are communicating. They learned them even before they could speak fully.

From 3-6 years children are learning much about their own culture. They may be leaving home for the first time to go to pre-school and will be exposed to other people and other ways of doing things. The sensitive period for culture at this time focuses on 'the way to do things'. Whether it is taking off your shoes at the door or shaking hands when you meet someone, a child of three or four will be fascinated. He wants to know what is done and then insists on doing it all the time. He watches adults in shops, on the telephone, crossing the road, brushing their hair. He watches carefully when an adult takes the time to show him how exactly it is done. Then he meticulously tries to do it himself. He will get upset if not allowed to do it the 'right way'.

This is also a time when stories about the 'olden days' appeal to a child. He will prefer a story about your own childhood than a magical fairytale. Culture at this age is not about art museums and musical symphonies. Rather it is about the customs and background of the child's own family.

3.8.   Culture & the Prepared Environment 3-6

The sensitive period for culture is catered for in the Montessori prepared environment 3-6 years in two main areas.

Practical Life

The children are presented with exercises on caring for themselves or for the environment. These exercises will obviously relate to the culture they live in. Children in Norway will learn how to wax skis, while children in Spain may learn to put on their sun hats. Each will learn how to set the table for lunch according to local customs.

There are a group of Montessori practical life exercises called Grace and Courtesy. In these the children are taught in a precise fun way about the manners and courtesies of their society. They learn how to greet people, how to excuse themselves, how to close a door and so on. They love these exercises because of their need to know 'how things are done'. Little ceremonies, religious or related to nature, attract children of 3-6 years. Lighting candles is a great favourite.

The teachers will conduct their daily business about the classroom in a precise clear way which the children can follow. For example if there is a visitor to the Montessori school he will be greeted and invited in, according to the manners of the local culture.

Cultural Subjects

The children in a Montessori pre-school will use exercises and do projects on history, geography and nature as well as music and art. These will involve using beautiful sensorial materials which they can handle and enjoy. It also involves pictures, books and stories told by the teacher. There will be exciting stories about animals, other countries and the world long ago. They will listen to beautiful music and hear about famous composers. Maybe famous artists and their paintings will be the subject of class projects and individual activities. All these stories are backed up by real activities and attractive pictures so the children absorb what they hear. From this they develop a feeling of being comfortable with their own culture.

3.9. Other Sensitive Periods

There are many sensitive periods and there are different ways of interpreting sensitive periods. Dr. Montessori asked us to understand the principles behind sensitive periods rather than labelling each of them. People will interpret mini-stages of sensitive periods as full sensitive periods and that is quite alright. You may talk about many other aspects of development as sensitive periods. For example you might say that a child has a sensitive period for reality in the time when they prefer reality to fantasy. You might also interpret the period of refining the senses (3-6 years) as a sensitive period. Although sensitive periods as Dr. Montessori described them are confined to the first six years, you will be able to see similar stages in later life. For example a child of 5-7 years is particularly interested in being a member of a group or a 'gang'. Or a twenty-five year old is particularly interested in developing his career while a fifty year old may be more interested in looking into his inner life.

3.10. Adults & Sensitive Periods

Children all over the world follow a general pattern for sensitive periods but of course there will be some variations. Even Montessori teachers or trained child development experts will not know exactly when to expect a sensitive period. Adults must learn to observe. When they see things happening which indicate that a sensitive period is happening, they must immediately concentrate on removing obstacles and in providing support to the natural process of learning.

> *"Such assistance will not consist in forming the child since this task belongs to nature herself, but in a delicate respect for the outward manifestations of this development and in providing those means necessary for his formation which he cannot obtain by his own efforts alone." (Montessori, M., The Secret of Childhood, Chapter, Psychic Development, 1966)*

We cannot get it right every time but by supporting the nature of the child, we will make both him and ourselves happier. Above all we must avoid trying to work against the sensitive periods just because we believe that 'a child must learn to conform'. We must be aware of the wonders of nature that are taking place.

4.

THE SENSITIVE PERIOD FOR

MOVEMENT 3-6

Movement and language are two of the principal sensitive periods for 3-6 year olds. The sensitive period for order 3-6 years is also very important but is developed in greater detail under Sensorial Education.

4.1. Overview of Movement

Dr. Montessori placed great emphasis on movement as being the basis of all learning especially in the first three years of life. She stressed that without movement the child was limited in her ability to seek out and receive the necessary sensory stimulation for all development. Lack of freedom of movement also restricts the child's powers of self-expression and interaction with others.

"Mental work ought to be accompanied by sensations of truth and beauty, which reanimate it, and by movements which bring ideas into play and leave their traces in the external world, where men ought to be giving each other mutual help." (Montessori, M., The Discovery of the Child, Chapter, Education in Movement, 1966)

Dr. Montessori also placed great emphasis on the use of the hand in learning. She said all animals could walk but it was the human ability to use the hand for precise tasks that led to the development of civilisation. She talked about how man's "hands under the guidance of his intellect transform this environment and thus enable him to fulfil his mission in the world." (Montessori, M., The Secret of Childhood, Chapter - The Hand, 1966). In her observations of children Dr. Montessori saw that the adult restriction on children's freedom to touch and handle things was the cause of so many developmental problems, both intellectual and emotional.

"..the child's intelligence can develop to a certain level without the help of his hand. But if it develops with his hand, then the level it reaches is higher, and the child's character is stronger." (Montessori, M., The Absorbent Mind, Chapter - Intelligence and the Hand, 1988)

The long infancy of the human being allows the cerebellum to develop after birth. While this part of the brain is growing and the infant is learning about movement, the psyche is developing at the same time. The fact that muscular and psychic movement develop in co-operation with each other cannot be overstressed. This is why Dr. Montessori said that freedom of movement was an absolute right of every child.

"A child's movements are not due to chance. Under the direction of his ego he builds up the necessary coordination for organised movement. At the expense of countless intervening experiences, his ego coordinates, organises and unifies his organs of expression with his developing psyche." (Montessori, M., The Secret of Childhood, Chapter, The Hand, 1966)

Dr. Montessori's charts on movement and the hand in *The Absorbent Mind* are important reference points. (These charts are usually found with the chapters The Importance of Movement and The Intelligence and the Hand) (Montessori, M., The Absorbent Mind, 1988) Some of the ages given by Dr. Montessori may be adjusted slightly but overall the same pattern applies to all children today.

	The Hand	**Equilibrium - [Large Motor Movement]**
0-2 months	The child has an instinctive prehension and grips anything which touches its hand.	Very little control except to move limbs
2-6 months	Learns to grasp and studies hand.	Control of head - can lift head and shoulders by 3 months.
6-12 months	Purposeful grasping of objects. Chooses objects. Repetition of activities. Uses hand in climbing and crawling.	Rapid development of cerebellum Sits if helped - 6 months Sits alone; belly crawl - 7-8 months Stands if helped; creeps - 8-10 months Walks with help 10-12 months
1-1.5 year	First efforts at 'work'. Uses the hands to do particular tasks. Uses hands in climbing. Starts to lift heavy object.	Walks alone 12-16 months Climbs small heights
1.5-2 years	Practises activities with the hand. Moves things about with purpose and intention. Starts to do tasks like dusting, washing up, laying the table.	Carries heavy objects - effort and balance ['Little porters'] Climbs stairs; Starts little running steps
2-3 years	Uses hands to do many everyday activities, always leading to independence	Runs; Uses entire body in various movements; Takes long walks
3-4.5 years	Refines the use of the hand. Repetition of activities until a fine precision is reached	Skips; Refining energetic movement Likes to use whole body in activities
4.5-6 years	Uses hand to act upon the world and get things done. Refines precision of hand to write, sew, paint, cut, throw ball and other tasks of the civilised human being	Refinement of gymnastic movements (using of whole body in a variety of positions); Runs faster; Climbs with precision.

4.2. Refinement of Large Motor Movement

Dr. Montessori stressed balance as an important part of the development of large motor movement. She pointed out that the cerebellum (an organ at the base of the brain that controls balance) is developing in stages going through sitting, standing and then walking. Children will strive constantly to get away from the restrictions of adults to climb, creep, walk and run. They will be upset if the adult tries to help them. Children start to refine large motor movement from as early as their second year and will continue doing so for many years. By four years they can run, jump and skip. Children will practise movements endlessly. We see children of seven and eight years playing games like hop-scotch or balancing on branches of trees. Children do not stop refining movement at six years so obviously the sensitive period for movement spills over into the next stage of development.

In the period 3-6 years children steadily refine and improve their large motor movements. They need freedom of movement to do this. Space to run and climb outdoors will be necessary. Indoors they will need floor space to spread themselves around while they work and play. Furniture used for children should be child-sized and easy to move We do not have to teach children about movement but we do have to remove obstacles in the environment and in our own attitudes to freedom of movement. Adults need to be aware that restriction of movement will cause emotional stress because the sensitive period is being blocked.

4.3. Detail & Small Objects

Closely allied to the sensitive period for movement is the sensitive period for detail and small objects. This generally lasts from 1-4 years. A child of 1 year spots every little insect on the floor. The child of 3 years will look at a big bright beautiful picture and will ignore everything except a little mouse sitting under a leaf. When a child focuses on physical objects that are small she practises and refines her pincer grip, using thumb and forefinger. This will be a most important skill in later learning. She also practises her eye focus. When a child focuses on detail in a picture, she is practising being observant and this also will be very important in later learning.

4.4. Refinement of the Hand

In the first three years the child has learned to do basic tasks with her hand. Precision of movement will start to attract her so deeply that she will repeat tasks until she gets them right. Dr. Montessori saw the hand as being significant in the development of the human race. She stressed that the use of the hand was intimately connected with the development of the intellect. The 3-6 year old is working to make conscious what was unconscious. Dr. Montessori believed that most of this was done through work with the hands.

In the period 3-6 years the adult must provide many opportunities for the child to do real tasks which involve the hand. Adults should not be impatient with children who are slow to fasten their shoes. The intense concentration between eye, hand and intellect that goes on when these shoes are being fastened is a most important learning experience. The sensitive period for movement is driving the child to practise fine motor movements. If the child is constantly denied opportunities to do this, she will become frustrated and angry. She will be driven to find other things to do with her hands and may turn to destructive activities. We as adults are responsible for removing obstacles and providing opportunities for practice when required.

4.5. Movement & Safety

The task of the Montessori adult in preparing an environment, indoor or outdoor, is to make a safe environment which does not take away the child's right to freedom and independence. This demands that adults analyse each part of the environment and question every traditional safety measure. It does not mean that Montessori environments should in any way be unsafe. Rather, Montessorians would claim that the children are safer because they have been taught how to use things carefully.

Most pre-schools use good scissors nowadays but Montessori schools introduced them many years ago. Montessori teachers went out and found sharp but rounded scissors. They then kept them away from the children until they were ready to give a full and precise lesson on how to hold and use a scissors. Montessori schools also have rules about where and how a scissors may be used. The children are all in a sensitive period for order and will follow these guidelines if given in an orderly manner.

In the same way, a Montessori school will not forbid children to climb. They will show the children how to climb. If a tree or frame is unsafe to climb, the teacher will remove it. To put oneself in the position of having to forbid and to correct is not the right way for a Montessori adult. Let the lessons and the environment be the guides.

Should there be an accident, and there are always some little accidents, it is important that teachers let all the children see what is happening, so that they may learn by experience how to take necessary precautions. If one child hurts another, whether by accident or not, the aggressive child should help to take care of the injured child. It offers an opportunity to make amends.

4.6. Movement & the Prepared Environment

Freedom of movement is built into the design of the Montessori prepared environment. The furniture is designed and laid out to give space to move with ease about the classroom. Everything is laid out so that children can take and replace them without adult help.

Montessori exercises in every category are designed to give practice in refinement of movement. Eye hand co-ordination is encouraged by the precision required to handle objects. The teacher presents these objects using precise hand movement that the child can follow. Exercises like sewing, cutting, folding are encouraged to develop refinement of hand movement. Large motor movement is refined by children moving their own chairs and tables as needed. There are also exercises specially designed for refining these movements, for example 'Walking on the Line' and 'The Silence Game'. If you enter a Montessori classroom you will see that there is much movement. Everybody is moving about in a natural way, learning as they go.

4.7. Dr. Montessori & Physical Education

Dr. Montessori argued against physical education for pre-school children. However, given the enormous advances in the meaning of the words physical education, we may have to reinterpret that view. In Dr. Montessori's day physical education was army style gymnastics. Her objection to physical education as known in her own day was based on two simple points, closely related to each other.

- All people, children and adults, would be better off doing ordinary tasks in their lives than doing artificial exercises to keep fit. She would not have liked the 'keep fit' classes and gyms in our society to-day. Dr. Montessori thought we would all be better to go out and dig our gardens and clean our houses. Part of her reason for thinking this was that it was better for human dignity to do one's own 'practical life' tasks.

- The other argument that Dr. Montessori had against gymnastics for children was that mind and body should always develop together. Therefore it made no sense to do exercises for the development of the body alone. Rather she thought we ought to allow the children to move about naturally while they did their learning. In *The Discovery of the Child* she refers to the Red Man and the White Man. These were the nervous system and the circulation/ digestive system. She described the muscular system as the system that connected these two systems, "the lofty functions of the life of relationships" and she said if we just exercised muscles in a bodily manner we would have "degraded [the organs for the expressions of the mind] to the mere task of helping the blood to travel more quickly [...]" (Montessori, M. The Discovery of the Child, Chapter, Education in Movement, 1966) Dr. Montessori believed that muscles were so intimately connected with our minds and our self-control that they deserved more respect than they were commonly given.

Dr. Montessori had many ideas for physical education. In her very first book, *The Montessori Method*, written in 1911, (Montessori, M., The Montessori Method, 1964) she outlined ideas for a low level plank of wood for the children to walk on. She also recommended wires like fencing for the children to walk on, whilst holding another wire. She strongly advocated in all her books that children do their own practical life activities as far as possible, moving chairs and tables, sweeping floors and gardening.

Nowadays physical education experts agree with Dr. Montessori about combining mental and physical activity. In fact they will claim that physical education helps mental development as children learn to remember sequences of movement and to control their muscles. They also point out great social and emotional benefits in a well planned physical education programme. Based on her overall views we can surmise that Dr. Montessori would have agreed with them.

The Montessori teacher to-day has the task of developing physical education within a framework of Montessori principles. He must firstly ensure that he understands the Montessori principles of movement. Then research into modern ideas and equipment for physical education will broaden his ideas. However before he takes on any particular exercise or apparatus, he ought to analyse its worth in the context of the whole Montessori philosophy. Never should a teacher think of physical education, indoor or outdoors, as 'outside the Montessori time'. Every moment of the day is Montessori time in a Montessori school.

4.8. Children's Games 3-6

Between the ages of 3 and 6 years children love games but if you examine the social nature of the child, you will realise that certain games are not suitable. Team games, such as football, hockey and so on, involve a group approach and interaction which is beyond the capability of the child under 6 years. In fact team games are really only suitable from about 8 years when children have learned the basics of co-operating in groups.

Games involving skills, such as throwing and catching, using a bat, using a skipping rope, will not be suitable. In the refinement of movement between 3 and 6 years, the children will develop skills which will lead to the ability to use bats and throw a ball. In the meantime a game which involves too much skill will quickly become boring for the child under 6 years. Skill games become more relevant after 6 years.

Games involving competition are of little relevance to children under 6 years. By about 7 years the involvement and interest in group activities will have helped the child to develop a sense of fun in competition. The child under 6 is too self-centred in her development to be able to understand anything like competition. When another child wins she will think that she has been denied something that she wants and/or needs. It can lay a sense of great insecurity to introduce competition before children have reached the emotional maturity necessary to cope with it.

Now that we have isolated the games not suitable for children under 6 years, let us look at what they do like and gain from. Games involving spontaneous tumbling, rolling, running, jumping and fun will always appeal to the pre-school child. Games with rhymes, songs, clapping and dancing will be popular. Large soft balls or bean bags are suitable for this age but the children may have more fun chasing after the bean bag than throwing or catching it. Games of going under or over, in or out, making circles or arches are fun and they help language development.

You will find that some of the traditional street games appeal to pre-school children but the teacher ought to examine these carefully as most street games are designed for the older child. An aware Montessori teacher will be able to adapt games using the Montessori principles. Dr. Montessori herself observed the older children as they hopped along the pavement, trying to miss every line, or perhaps trying to walk on every line. She then adapted that for the pre-school children and invented the 'Walking on the Line' exercise.

Overall children of 3-6 years should not be asked to take part in group activities for long periods. They prefer individual activities or games where they act spontaneously together. Good outdoor play equipment will provide the exercise they need. Children benefit socially from games but the Montessori teacher must decide what games to introduce, based on the social nature of the child at that age. He must remember that, under 6 years, development of the self is of more importance than the group.

4.9. Physical Education & Outdoors

All day is 'Montessori time' in a Montessori school. We must never make the mistake of thinking that Montessori is only the lessons presented inside the classroom. We need to apply the same principles to all activities from reception in the morning to the moment of going home.

If we want a physical education programme we must have a prepared environment. Physical education indoors may be in the classroom or may be in a gymnastics hall. In either case the environment must be prepared for the children. The outdoor playing area must also be a prepared environment. Montessori teachers need to give time and thought to planning it. The Montessori classroom will have a line for walking on and will have the space for free movement. Chairs and tables are made so the children can lift them. You may be planning indoor physical education classes in the classroom. In that case you will need to clear a large space away from the normal working area. You will confuse the children if you change the 'code' of movement in the classroom just because it is gymnastic time. Moving all the chairs and tables out will be sufficient to impress the children that this is a special time. The moving of the furniture will be physical education in itself.

If you are lucky enough to have a gymnastics hall, make sure it is prepared for the pre-school children. Remove or cover equipment which you do not wish them to use. Then, before you let the children play freely, show them the safety procedures for the equipment. As with all Montessori exercises, show how to use beforehand, rather than having to correct the children later.

Apply the same principles outdoors as indoors. Take away anything which is not in use. Do not introduce outdoor activities which need the help of an adult all the time. Encourage independence. Show children how to use things properly and then stand back. Have the correct utensils for outdoors. Gardening equipment, sweeping brushes, shovels should be cut to child height. They must have a proper storage place and children must know how to use them, how to take them out and how to put them away. If, for example, you wish sweeping leaves to be an activity in the autumn, you need to have a brush, a collection container and a place to put the collected leaves. The lesson should be presented in the same way as any other practical life exercise.

Allow spontaneous play outdoors but also have some structured activities. These do not have to be group activities. It may be that the teacher shows one or more children how to use something or carry out a new activity each day. The teacher can play a game with the group for a short period each day or just play with a small group as appropriate at the time.

The important points to remember are that environments must be prepared and Montessori principles should be followed whether indoors or outdoors.

4.10. The Role of the Adult Outdoors

The functions of the adult outdoors are:

- To prepare and then keep the environment and the equipment within it

- To observe the children and to change the environment according to what was observed

- To prepare activities to help the children to become independent

- To preserve order within the environment

- To allow freedom but within structured guidelines. These will be less structured than indoors because the space is larger and because the activities involve large motor movement rather than fine motor movement

- To present activities and then not to interfere unless absolutely necessary

- To present rather than to correct

- To watch over safety with an emphasis on 'showing how' rather than 'protecting from'.

- To guide the children socially by offering a good example in behaviour, by presenting outdoor courtesy lessons to the children and by encouraging spontaneous interaction between children

The teacher outdoors has a role quite similar to that indoors. The difficulty lies in the fact that most teachers either think outdoors is boring or that it is a resting time for teachers. It challenges the Montessori teacher to apply Montessori principles outdoors. It requires a thorough knowledge of the principles to do this. Many new teachers assume that it is easier than indoors but in fact the outdoors is more difficult for the teacher. Indoors the teacher has the support of the traditional Montessori materials. Outdoors the teacher must look deeply into the Montessori principles and develop his own ideas and rules.

5.

THE SENSITIVE PERIOD FOR

LANGUAGE 3-6

> Children up to 6 years are actually creating themselves and as part of that creation they are creating language.

5.1. Overview of Language

Language is a left brain activity which means it is controlled by the rational mind. There is also a creative side to language. Adults and older children use language creatively. Language is one of the most fascinating parts of child development and Dr. Montessori has written much about the wonder of watching how language develops in a child.

Sensitive periods are a support to the development of the child in particular areas. Let us take an overview of language development from birth to six years to highlight the importance of the changing focus of the sensitive periods. This will be relevant when preparing language development activities for a Montessori class. Refer to the chart on the development of language in *The Absorbent Mind* (this chart is usually found in the chapter How Language Calls the Child) (Montessori, M., 1988).

47

0-2 months

New born babies are comforted by voices, especially their mother's. The only noticeable sounds they make are hiccupping and crying. We know they are absorbing language because they start reacting to speech during this period.

2-6 months

The child starts to 'coo'. Dr. Montessori uses the phrase 'separate nebulae', meaning little unconnected sounds. At about four months a child studies the adult's mouth intently and discovers that that is where the sounds are coming from.

6 months to 1 year

This is the time of repeated babbling. The child practices again and again, trying every possible sound. Towards the end of this period the child abandons the sounds which he has not been hearing in the environment and starts to make words belonging to his own language. By 9 or 10 months the child's sounds have some meaning, even if we do not always understand it. By 11 or 12 months he is uttering his first intentional words. The child understands most simple statements made to him by the time he is 1 year old.

1 year to 1.5 years

In this period the child practises little words and starts to name things. He starts to fuse words to create meaning, for example, "mog" to mean "my dog". Sometimes he babbles meaningfully and thinks everybody understands him. His understanding is far more advanced than speech. This can be a difficult time for the child as he thinks that he is understood as well as he understands. He becomes frustrated with adults who cannot follow his meaning.

1.5 to 2 years

Language increases rapidly in this period. Adjectives, verbs and prepositions are added to the nouns. Phrases of a few words appear three to four months before the second birthday. At around 2 years of age there is a sudden 'explosion into speech' and we hear the child making little sentences using correct syntax. Sometimes the child talks all day for a few weeks as he practises this new skill of speaking.

2 to 2.5 years

The child can now talk, language is complete. Over this six months the variety and completeness of phrases and sentences is improved. By 2.5 years the child can express his thoughts in language.

2.5 to 6 years

This is a time for the refinement of language. The child practises words and in the first part of this phase we will hear him using complicated words with all the sounds complete but in the wrong sequence. This is a sensitive period for vocabulary. The child is attracted to words and wants to learn more and more of them. This sensitivity to words means that it is an ideal time to learn to read. (See below for details.)

Dr. Montessori asked us to pay particular attention to this wonderful process of language development because language is central to all human development and social life.

"Language lies at the root of that transformation of the environment that we call civilisation." (Montessori, M., The Absorbent Mind, Chapter, Some Thoughts on Language, 1988)

5.2. Sensitive Period for Vocabulary

Between the ages of 2.5 and about 5 or 6 years, the child is intensely interested in words. He wants to learn words. When we give him new words he tries to use them in his own speech. He wants the words for animals, cars, trees, people's names, colours and everything in his experience. Dr. Montessori started to give children technical words for geometry and science and they looked for more. Adults should use a rich vocabulary with children and they will absorb it quickly. Children hear words in their environment and then Dr. Montessori's three period lesson can be used to present the words precisely, ensuring that the child has got the correct pronunciation and correct meaning. Vocabulary increases tenfold in this period.

5.3. Sensitive Period for Composition of Words

One of the most interesting things to observe in this sensitive period for vocabulary is the way a child takes in the composition of a word. Sometimes he hears a long difficult word and uses it wrongly. Listen carefully and you will notice that he gets every sound of the word but puts them in the wrong sequence. An example in English is "hospital" which is mispronounced as "hospital", or "particular" mispronounced as "parlitucar". This shows that the child must indeed have a special sensitivity to words in order to absorb so much detail.

This sensitivity is what led Dr. Montessori to realise that this was an ideal time to learn to write and read. It makes it easier for children to compose and write words than to read them. This was the basis for Dr. Montessori's revolutionary 'writing before reading' system.

Children in a Montessori pre-school will learn vocabulary by a three-period lesson. Words which they have heard in the environment will be presented in a precise way isolating the meaning of the word and the exact pronunciation. The children love these words. This demonstrates that children are not only interested in the words and their meaning but they are also attracted to learning the precise pronunciation. The sensitive period leads them to listen carefully to the sounds and exactly how they are put together. It is this sensitivity which allows them to learn vocabulary with such ease.

5.4. Writing before Reading

Dr. Montessori was famous for her approach to the teaching of reading and writing. She believed that writing came naturally before reading. Note that within the term writing she included word building, or composing words, with the movable alphabet. The children in the first Children's House started to write spontaneously one day. They apparently did not know what they had written. This is an important aspect of what happened. Teachers sometimes forget and try to get children to interpret what they have produced, that is read. Reading back is not relevant at this stage. They are producing words with pencil, chalk or cut-out letters in the way they paint at that age. The process is the point of interest. The end result is of little value to them. They are truly in a creative process. They are creating words. As Dr. Montessori realised, they write (or create words) before they read.

The core of Dr. Montessori's method is based on the fact that this is a sensorial method for teaching writing and reading. It is not necessarily easy to learn to read or write before 6 years using other methods. The materials must be tactile and look attractive. They need to involve activity. It also relies on the child being free to make spontaneous choices. That is why the child is firstly introduced to exercises in practical life and sensorial education, gradually building an awareness of the level of choice available. When it comes to language exercises it is necessary to make the activities attractive and fun so that the children are drawn to them.

There should be an array of activities to practise writing and word-building. These must be presented in an attractive way by the teacher. The teacher must not try to *teach* in the old fashioned sense. When the child knows the sounds of the letters and knows how to use the materials he will spontaneously start to build or write words. We need to play many games to encourage word analysis. These are fun to the child as he is in a sensitive period for words. We also need many exercises for strengthening the hand to allow the child to develop the ability to write. Following a period of months practising word building or writing the child will find reading quite easy. It is not a conscious process of learning to read. Rather the whole process goes on in a sensorial unconscious manner. Suddenly the child finds he can read. It may seem like a slow process to an onlooker because there is so much preparation work but it is an enjoyable and thorough method, based on the child's natural needs at that age.

5.5. Sensitive Period for Composition of Sentences

At about 5 years of age another interesting development in the sensitive period for language takes place. Children become interested in sentences and how they are structured. While they absorbed grammar and syntax when they learned to talk, they now focus with precision on the exact way this is done. You can observe them putting together more complex sentences, using adverbs and adjectives in different ways. They start to play word games like 'I Spy' (a game of trying to guess objects in the environment when only given the first letter). Grammar exercises involving moving words around within sentences will appeal and the Montessori grammar materials will provide exactly that for the 5 year old. They are attracted to activities that make it fun to explore which adjective or which adverb to use. The sense of humour that a child develops around 5 years will add to the fun of this language exploration. A simple choice of "the red hen" or "the red man" will be a source of much fun and even more learning.

In the last stages of the sensitive period for language (which may last until about seven years) the child evolves an interest in using the words he has acquired and exploring many ways of composing sentences with them. He is not only creating words but he is creating sentences. This is indeed a wonderful way to be prepared to move into a world of learning at the age of 6 or

7 years. Most learning comes through language in one way or another. In order to take advantage of this a child's language ought to be well finished and quite sophisticated. Nature has prepared the child to do this. All we have to do is to observe the child, remove obstacles and take advantage of these special sensitive periods.

PART 2:

MONTESSORI IN ACTION

FOR

THE PRE-SCHOOL CHILD

6.

CULTURE & PRACTICAL LIFE FOR THE

PRE-SCHOOL CHILD

The central part of cultural education in a Montessori pre-school is brought about through a series of activities called Practical Life.

6.1. Practical Life 3-6

The child of 3-6 years is ready for many practical activities. She wants to be a part of the enclosed society that she finds in her home or at pre-school. These activities are the main tools to help her to learn the skills she needs in her own culture.

Practical Life exercises are presented to the child at 2.5 or 3 years of age and continue right through to adolescence. However the time when children work most with practical life activities is between 2.5 and 4 years of age.

A practical life activity in the 3-6 years classroom is usually a refinement of a skill that the child has already tried in his first three years. There will also be completely new skills. Practical life exercises are central to the Montessori method. There are some important educational principles behind these activities.

6.2.   What is Practical Life?

- A practical life exercise is an activity related to skills which are part of everyday normal social life.

- All practical life activities must be demonstrated by the adult in a positive manner. Adults show how to do the activity and do not correct previous errors. They should demonstrate the correct behaviour as an objective lesson.

- Practical life is a child's work. There is a difference between an adult's purpose in work and a child's. The adult wants to get the task completed, the child wants to create his personality. She works for the sake of the work itself.

- Practical life exercises are the key to the young child's culture, opening doors to the ways in which people in her own society carry out a wide range of everyday activities.

- Practical life exercises are the basis for all later education, giving children the skills they need to learn about other things as they grow.

6.3.   The Basic Principles of Practical Life

Reality - all items must be real; all activities must be real, no make believe; use natural materials as far as possible; use the best of everything for the child.

Independence - activities must lead the child towards independence; exercises must be graded in step-by-step progression according to the age and ability of the child.

Analysis of sequence of movement - each step of the exercise must be analysed and planned in minute detail by the adult before presentation to the child.

Order - activities must satisfy the need for order; order must be built into the materials and into the presentation.

Control - the activities should include features which highlight error, thereby acting as an inbuilt control of error allowing for self-correction of mistakes. This feature will also act as a point of interest in the exercise.

Repetition - it must be possible to repeat activities as often as the child needs to; the activities must be available to the child at all times; the exercises must allow for the child's inner cycle of activity.

6.4. The Purposes of Practical Life

- **Independence** - each activity will give the child practice in the skills necessary to become independent. "Help me to do it alone" is the cry of the child!

- **Cultural awareness** – giving the child understanding of her culture in the immediate locality and her own country; sense of belonging.

- **Social adaptability** - helps the child to gain awareness of the **needs of others**; sense of responsibility.

- **Self-knowledge** - mental development; self-confidence; self-esteem.

- **Control of movement** – helps to refine movement (gross and fine); physical development, eye-hand co-ordination; spatial awareness.

- **Concentration** - self-control; building up an **outer work-cycle.**

Practical life has many purposes. Practical life is different in every Montessori school. It is based on the culture in which the child is living. It is one of the ways in which she is able to practice being a member of her own group in society.

6.5. Categories of Practical Life

Practical Life activities are divided into three main categories.
There are many preliminary activities to prepare the hand. These are occasionally given a category of their own but they are usually connected with the first category, Care of the Environment.

* Care of the Environment – activities such as pouring, cleaning, washing.

* Care of the Self – activities such as hand washing, dressing/undressing.

* Grace & Courtesy - activities in graceful movement such as carrying a chair and activities in courtesy such as greeting a visitor.

6.6. Culture as Part of Social Life

Apart from language there are many other cultural and social modes, differing from one country to another, from one race to another, even from one gender to another. Dr. Montessori believed the child absorbed her culture. She talks about how *"the child, thanks to his peculiar psyche, absorbs the customs and habits of the land in which he lives, until he has formed the typical individual of his place and time." (Montessori, M., The Absorbent Mind, 1988)*

What do we mean by culture when talking about a pre-school child? Culture is often interpreted as art, music and literature. But there is a much wider interpretation of the word and it is that interpretation which we apply to the child. Culture refers to all the mannerisms, habits, customs, tastes, likes and dislikes of a group of people. Some peoples use many hand gestures, others are more reserved. Certain groups like to talk a lot while others prefer silence. The things we grew up with as children became a part of us and we feel at home with them at a deep level. We learned most of these before 6 years of age.

6.7. Sowing Seeds of Interest in the Cosmos

The child develops a sense of deep interest in the wide world from about 6 years. The child under 6 years is more interested in the immediate environment. However, this younger child is still receiving some experiences of the wider world. From hearing about America, to listening to Mozart, to looking at the stars, the child will absorb little bits of information about the cosmos. These may only be of interest for the younger child in so far as they affect her daily life. For example she may ask "Will the stars fall down on me in the night?" The information about the cosmos that is absorbed will be held in the child's mind, waiting for the right moment to germinate. This will happen when she is over 6 years, probably on the day that someone reminds her of an earlier experience. When she is studying something about galaxies at seven years, she will react and say, "But I love the stars". She may or may not remember looking at stars when she was four but the seed of interest is still there in her mind. Seeds sown at any time during childhood may germinate in adolescence or even in adulthood. Dr. Montessori said that we should […]

> *"[…]broadcast […] the maximum number of seeds of interest. These will be held lightly in the mind, but will be capable of later germination." (Montessori, M., To Educate the Human Potential, Chapter, The Six-Year-Old Confronted with the Cosmic Plan, 1973)*

6.8. Belonging to the Universe

Culture is presented in a Montessori school at this age to help the child gain a sense of place in the universe, a sense of place in time and space and a sense of place within the living kingdom. It is all based on the child herself and on her immediate experience. She will have gained some sense of her place in the family and the immediate community before 3 years. Now, between 3 and 6 years, she can start to get a sense of belonging to the whole universe. She needs this to ground her in the reality, which is so attractive to her in this period.

When we talk about animals and animal kingdoms to the children 3-6 years, we look for the mammals and point out that we are mammals too. When we look at the globe the child wants to know where her own continent, her own country, her own town is. The most exciting part of the story of the time-line of life is the little red strip at the end when people first arrived on Earth. Children love stories about the world but it must always come back to where she is at just now.

6.9. Activity in Cultural Exercises

Cultural exercises in pre-school should involve activity. Many Montessori teachers make the mistake of presenting wonderfully exciting lessons, but forget the follow-up independent activities for the children. The children need activities to help them to absorb the information that went with the inspiring story. These activities may take the form of matching cards, pouring water or puzzle maps. They learn to pour water into land and water forms, to feel the sandpaper globe in a sensorial way, to roll out the long timeline and to match pictures to it by colour.

The activities may also be in the form of drawing, painting or making a model. You may have stencils for the children to draw or clay to make animals. You may organise a group project for the children on a topic such as 'The Birds in our Garden' or 'Dinosaurs'. You will guide the project and the children will take part in different activities. This level of activity is suitable for the older pre-school children of 5-6 years. It is not advisable to involve the 3-4 year olds in too many group activities as their focus is still on individual development. Projects may be a bit abstract for them. They want only sensorial reality.

6.10. Culture for the Older Child

By presenting culture as explained here we prepare the ground for Cosmic Education which is used in all Montessori schools for children 6-12 years. For the older child the cultural subjects (biology, history, geography, art, music) form a major part of the cosmic curriculum. Language and mathematics are also integrated. The cosmic curriculum is based on the wonder and beauty and the interconnectedness of everything in the universe.

The imagination is the driving force for learning for the child 6-12 years. Inspiring facts and figures about the universe, inspiring pictures, books and activities form the central core of inspiration for the imagination.

> *"These subjects must be presented so as to touch the imagination of the child, and make him enthusiastic, and then add fuel to the burning fire that has been lit."*
> *(Montessori, M., To Educate the Human Potential, Chapter, The Right Use of the Imagination, 1973)*

Cosmic education, for children 6-12 years, is the way we teach all subjects, relating them to one another. An apple on a tree may lead to the study of mathematics or grammar and that may lead to studying the Egyptians. The main focus of the curriculum is inspiration.

In the 3-6 years period we are preparing for Cosmic Education. We sow seeds of interest and help the child to ground himself in the reality of where she belongs in the big scheme of things.

7.

SENSORIAL EDUCATION

Sensorial education is about helping the child to become more aware of the sensorial impressions he receives.

7.1. Sensorial Impressions or Sensorial Education

Sensorial education is not about improving the senses. It is not about increasing the sensorial impressions a child receives. It is about helping the child to know more what he senses.

Sensorial impressions are what we receive from the world around us. We may smell a flower, hear a bird sing, see a beautiful sunrise, taste exotic food or feel the touch of a newborn baby's hand. We may see an ugly dump, hear a road drill or smell a sewer. Whatever we sense it affects us, we take it in through our senses and the message goes to our brain where we have a reaction to the sensation received. That is our human condition and unless there is some damage to one of the systems, we do this throughout our lives.

Sensorial education aims to help a child know better what he is sensing. The aim is *not* to make him smell better or to hear better. Rather it is to be more aware of what he is smelling and more aware of what he is hearing. Two people can smell the same flower, get the same smell and have a totally different reaction. One person may rub his nose and just keep reading the paper. The other may stop everything to savour the beautiful smell, it touches his soul. In fact you probably recognise the situation where you stop in wonder one day because you have seen a beautiful tree. You have been passing that tree every morning for a year and never noticed. Something catches your eye that day and you suddenly know what you are seeing. Dr. Montessori believed that 3-6 years was the best time for this education to take place.

"The period of life which lies between three and six years is a period of rapid psychical growth and building up the sensorial mental faculties. The child of that age is developing his senses; his attention is therefore directed towards the observation of his surroundings." (Montessori, M., The Discovery of the Child, Chapter, Education of the Senses, 1966)

7.2. Refinement of the Senses

Refinement of the senses is one of the aims of sensorial education. Note it is not about refining the actual sense. It is about refining the corresponding mental part of that sense.

A little girl of four years embarrassed her mother wherever they went in public places, on buses or in shops. She sniffed and said 'What is that smell?'. She could smell much better than her mother could and noticed whenever a person had strong body odour! She just loved the smelling jars in her Montessori class and had refined her sense of smell very well. Many years later she still has a very sensitive sense of smell.

It is now well proven that children exposed to music in the womb will react positively to that music later in life. This is a love of a certain sensory stimulus. Sensorial education aims to refine the senses in a more exact way than that. It aims to present sensory stimuli, smells, colours, shapes, sounds, tastes, in a way that helps the child to compare them, notice subtle differences and *become more aware.* In that way his senses are refined.

Another advantage of working with the senses at a young age is that sensory problems can be detected. For example, children with slight hearing loss will be unable to detect differences in the sound boxes. If you as a Montessori teacher notice this problem in a child, advise the parents to get a hearing test for the child.

7.3. Sensorial Materials

Dr. Montessori designed a wide range of beautiful materials for sensorial education. These materials help the child to refine his awareness of sensorial impressions and support orderly intellectual development.

There are matching colour tablets, graded colour tablets, matching sound boxes, smelling jars, touch boards, graded cylinders, graded blocks and many more. This material will catch your eye when you enter a Montessori classroom. It is strikingly attractive.

Montessori materials, but in particular sensorial materials, should have certain characteristics according to Dr. Montessori. Let us examine these characteristics

Limitation: There should be a limit to the materials. There should never be more than one of each material. Children must learn to wait and to co-operate. Limits generally encourage the children to focus and give attention to the task in hand. In this way concentration is built up.

Isolation: We should teach only one thing at a time with the materials. It is distracting to present too many things together and is better to isolate concepts in order to encourage concentration on a particular thing. For example if you are presenting shape you must make sure that everything is the same colour.

Attraction: Material must attract the child. It should be beautiful, aesthetically pleasing and should be placed where it can be easily seen. It should call to the child, begging to be used. The teacher should not force the child to use it but leave it to his spontaneous choice. Remember that spontaneous choice is the way in which the child can answer his true inner needs.

"In the same way in a field, the petals of all the flowers are calling to other living things with their perfumes and their colours, but the insect chooses the flower which is made for him." (Montessori, M., The Discovery of the Child, Chapter, The Material for Development, 1966)

Order: Material should be orderly. The order in the material should act as a focus for the activity. The smooth running of the classroom will also depend on orderly materials being kept orderly by the children and by the teacher.

Activity: The material must provoke activity. It must be possible to do things with it. In fact it must cry out to be used. There should be something that can be moved, or changed. Activity is the best way to learn anything. It encourages exploration and discovery.

Control of Error: All Montessori materials should include a control of error. The control is quite clear in some materials. For example, the last cylinder will simply not fit in the last hole, or the last pair will not match, if a mistake has been made. In some instances the control may be visual and in a few cases it is the teacher who acts as the control. Control cards with the correct layout will act as controls for puzzles. As the children get older use master control cards, which have correct answers on them. Children refer to these to check their own work. The control of error is a point of interest in the exercise. The lack of adult interference is important because this is the process that builds up concentration.

7.4. Sensorial Mathematics and Language

Apart from sensorial materials above, Montessori included a range of activities for learning about mathematics and language in a sensorial way. They are not always referred to as sensorial materials but strictly speaking they belong in this category.

When Montessori presented writing, reading and mathematics to the children at 4 years of age, she presented them using sensorial materials because she knew the children could absorb concepts effortlessly if they were presented in this way. They are in a sensitive period for sensorial education and these materials use the absorbent mind to make it natural to learn writing, reading and mathematics.

Children in a Montessori school learn these subjects very early because they learn them in a very different manner from the way language and mathematics are traditionally taught. There are sandpaper numerals and letters for the children to feel. There are number rods to manipulate and a movable alphabet to create words. These are *materialised abstractions* as Dr. Montessori called them. The children are learning through their senses.

7.5. The Use of the Hand

Sensorial materials must be activity provoking. This activity is nearly always done with the hand. Dr. Montessori saw close connections between the use of the hand and the development of the intellect. Dr. Montessori believed that the hand was the developed instrument of the specially evolved brain of humans. The hand is the means by which humans make their mark on the world. Movement of the hand allows refinement that can lead to the child becoming a concert pianist, a heart surgeon, a seamstress or a physiotherapist. Yet this is always controlled by the brain. The co-operation of the hand and the brain working together is a key factor in intelligent behaviour.

Sensorial materials have many hidden side purposes that help to refine the use of the hand. Children prepare for holding a pen by grasping the cylinders in a particular way. They prepare for writing by feeling around geometric shapes. They develop a light sensitive touch for writing by feeling sandpaper touch boards. There are many other examples. At all times a Montessori teacher should be aware of ways in which the use of the hand can be refined.

The use of the hand is a means of developing concentration. Activity with the hand is a good means of learning and because of the special connection between the hand and the brain, it often happens that when a child is using his hand in an intricate, intense activity, he starts to concentrate deeply. This is the secret key to the success of Montessori schools. Sensorial materials are particularly well suited to the development of concentration. As Dr. Montessori said of an activity:

> *"The essential thing is for the task to arouse such an interest that it engages the child's whole personality."*
> *(Montessori, M., The Absorbent Mind, Chapter, The Child's Contribution, 1988)*

7.6. Making Conscious what was Unconscious

Another important factor of work with the hand is making conscious what was unconscious. The child starts to become aware of himself at about 2.5 years. Consciousness is emerging. He has the task of becoming conscious of all the concepts he has absorbed during his first years. Sensorial education allows the child to notice things he has already seen and to isolate qualities. This helps him to become conscious of what he has already taken in but stored unconsciously. He starts to understand the 'redness' of red. Then he is helped to hold the idea in his conscious mind through the activity and by giving it a name, 'red'. Language helps to hold conscious ideas.

Making conscious what was unconscious is done through activity or work, again usually with the hand. There are, of course, other parts of the body that help to make unconscious knowledge conscious. But the hand is the most active in making conscious what was unconscious.

7.7. An Alphabet of Impressions

Order is a required characteristic in sensorial materials. This is directly related to orderly intellectual development. The intellect must be put in order so that it is possible to find things, and find them quickly. How is this done?

Sensorial education allows the child to build a type of warp (the base you create to weave cloth on), or you might call it a framework. It is like a filing system. Not everything is in this system as yet. The child has to create the system and can then add to it throughout his life. It is created from the impressions that the child has accumulated so far in life. In fact, the child before three years is already creating some kind of order on his knowledge. Now, between 3 and 6 years, the child gives special attention to this task, putting his intellect in order. We say it is a sensitive period for mental (or intellectual) order.

This warp/ filing system is created by taking the information already acquired and setting up a system of relationships between them. Dr. Montessori explained that there were so many things in the universe that we could not possibly manage to know them all. However, there is a limit to the number of qualities that objects have so we can define the innumerable things and put them into a manageable format. When the Phoenicians invented the alphabet they created a similar system for language. Words were unlimited but sounds were not. Therefore, we could represent words using a limited number of letters. And so was invented the alphabet. Dr. Montessori said that sensorial education created 'an alphabet of impressions'.

> *"But the number of different objects in the world is infinite, while the qualities they possess are limited. These qualities are therefore like the letters of the alphabet which can make up an indefinite number of words." (Montessori,*

M., The Absorbent Mind, Chapter, Through Culture and the Imagination, 1988)

This 'alphabet' then becomes the framework for the child's knowledge of the world. It is the basis for all later thinking and creativity. From this filing system the child is able to access a wide range of sensorial qualities and use them to support his intelligence and his creative activities.

7.8. The Abstraction of Ideas

The actual process by which the child creates this warp in sensorial education is a part of the human intelligence and a feature of the sensitive period for order. If a child is not in Montessori school he will use objects in his environment to do this. It is his nature. Sensorial education is an additional orderly support to help the child in this rather large task.

If a child takes two blue and two red colour tablets and he lays them near each other on the table, it is the colour that jumps to the attention of the senses. Colour is isolated. Everything else about the tablets is the same. This in itself brings the concept of a quality to the child's attention. The 'redness' of red is apparent. Up to this the child's idea of red may just have meant red dresses or red shoes. Dr. Montessori called her sensorial apparatus 'materialised abstractions' (Montessori, M., The Absorbent Mind, Chapter, Through Culture and the Imagination, 1988)

In a similar manner the child can abstract ideas about other aspects of his environment. He will become aware of loudness, softness, roughness, smoothness. The child at this time is abstracting ideas about very basic concrete objects in his environment. There is nothing new here, just a new way of looking at familiar things. This is the ideal manner in which to start the process of intellectual abstraction.

7.9. Comparing & Discriminating

What happens when the child starts to work with the sensorial material? Let us return to the example of the colour tablets, two red and two blue. The child compares the four tablets. To start the process the teacher takes one red tablet, and asks for another like that. The child compares the red to the blues and to the other red. His attention is drawn to similarities and differences. Now he discriminates between the red and the blue. He recognises the difference and is aware of why he recognises a difference. His attention is drawn to the qualities.

This mental process seems obvious to us as adults. But we actually use exactly the same process when making very complicated abstract judgments throughout our lives. The intellectual basis for this skill was laid when we were three years old. Of course the child is not able to tell us about all of this, but awareness has begun. That is how all processes start

7.10. Language & Sensorial Education

Qualities are abstract notions. The child has just become aware of what a quality is. We can help him to hold on to this abstract idea by the use of language. Language is always useful in grounding abstract ideas. We give the child labels for these ideas. You may wonder how to present names for abstract ideas to a child. Remember that the material has already isolated the quality so for the child that colour tablet represents red.

We present the names of things by means of a three period lesson. The three period lesson is used for many things in the 3-6 years classroom. The child is in a sensitive period for extension and refinement of vocabulary and wants more and more words. Teaching the name of a quality is one purpose of the use of the three period lesson, it helps to fix abstract ideas by giving them labels.

Here is a brief summary of the three period lesson:

- The object (representing a quality) is isolated and the *teacher names it.*

- The *child* is asked to *identify* the object from amongst other objects, this is discrimination.

- The object is isolated and the *child names it.*

- If a child has a problem at any stage, the teacher does not help or correct. She simply goes back to the previous stage again.

7.11. A Basis for Imagination & Creativity

Sensorial education is a support for intellectual development. Many people mistakenly think that developing the intellect in an orderly way does not encourage creative development and imagination. Dr. Montessori argued that in fact such ordering of impressions was a basis for imagination and creativity.

The alphabet of impressions created by the child creates opportunities for him to create a large data bank of colours, sounds, shapes and much more. These are now readily available to the child as he creates his own ideas. Sensorial education also has the effect of making children interested in sensorial impressions. They love new colours, new sounds and new shapes. They love to feel things and explore the world about them. Sensorial education has created the basis for creativity. When the child comes to 6 years of age, his creativity will explode. He will be ready.

8.

FANTASY & IMAGINATION

Imagination is a power of the mind. It is the power that allows humans to go beyond the confines of their physical form and to be part of a wider world. It is the power that leads humans to create new ideas and new ways of living.

8.1. What is the Imagination?

"We often forget that imagination is a force for the discovery of truth. The mind is not a passive thing, but a devouring flame, never in repose, always in action." (Montessori, M., The Absorbent Mind, Chapter, Through Culture and the Imagination, 1988)

Dr. Montessori believed that it was important to understand that the imagination was an integral part of the human mind and of the human personality. She strongly disapproved of those who would separate the imagination from intelligence. She said that in that way we restricted what the imagination could do and we removed an inspiring power from the intelligence. Nowadays, even though we have made advances in our holistic way of thinking about education, there is still a tendency amongst some adults to see imagination as belonging to the so called 'creative' subjects, art, music, drama, literature. These same people tend to see mathematics, grammar, physics and other 'logical' subjects as being nothing to do with imagination. The truth is, imagination acts as powerfully when doing a geometric theorem as when painting a picture.

> *"The secret of good teaching is to regard the child's intelligence as a fertile field in which seeds may be sown, to grow under the heat of flaming imagination." (Montessori, M., To Educate the Human Potential, Chapter, The Right Use of the Imagination, 1973)*

8.2. Fantasy & the Young Child

Dr. Montessori had a reputation for being opposed to fantasy. In this context we should clarify that she used the word fantasy as being unreal thoughts, thoughts on things that did not happen. She did not object to the child creating objects of fantasy but she objected to the adult feeding the child somebody else's fantasy *instead of* feeding her exciting reality. She also had a problem with adults presenting fantasy to children without making it clear that it was fantasy.

Children under about 4 or 5 years confuse reality and fantasy. This may lead to a situation where children believe stories told to them and develop real fears about goblins, trolls and witches. The child is also being 'set up' for disappointment when she believes in magic fairies that cure all.

She pointed out that the young child loves reality and is in a sensitive period for reality. A child of three prefers to hear a story about the milkman than about a prince. It is important to respect this sensitive period while a child is in it. If you encourage fantasy when reality is already attractive you may lay the roots of someone who escapes from reality throughout her life.

8.3. Imitation & the Young Child

A child goes through a time of imitation around the time she is 1 or 2 years old. She plays 'house' or 'shop' or 'telephone'. She is imitating adults and role-playing. Dr. Montessori maintained that this was a stage of immaturity. The child of two does not have the skills or the resource to live real life and therefore imitates it. She said that when a child is allowed to carry out real activities she will stop most of the role-play. She prefers to set real tables, talk on real telephones and buy in a real shop. She therefore believed that imitation was something that was more common to children of 2 years and that they would grow beyond the need for this between 3 and 5 years as they acquired more and more power with their own lives. Of course it is true that children imitate at all ages but the role-play type of imitation is needed less as children get opportunities to do the 'real thing'. There will always be a place for role-play where children are unable to carry out activities or express feelings and needs by any other means. Dr. Montessori simply said it has its limitations.

Another point which Dr. Montessori makes about imitation is that before children imitate, they must form the power to imitate. She stresses the importance of the process of preparation of the skills or faculties underlying any activities of the child. In this case she suggests practical life activities to support this preparation.

> *"The important thing is that before the child can imitate, he must be prepared for doing so, and this preparation derives from the efforts he has been making. [...] The example set by adults only provides the aim, or motive for imitation. It does not produce a successful result. [...] The child [...] often improves on the examples set him."*
> *(Montessori, M., The Absorbent Mind, Chapter, Development and Imitation, 1988)*

8.4. Fantasy or Reality

Apart from the child's ability to understand fantasy, Dr. Montessori did not approve of giving too much fantasy in any event. She did not object to fantasy, but said it should never replace reality. To her, reality was fascinating and attractive. There were many exciting things in this world from milkmen to glaciers, which are more appealing than fantasy. For children who understand the difference between reality and fantasy, Dr. Montessori allowed fantasy, as long as we explained to the children that it was fantasy. Father Christmas and the tooth fairy would not meet Dr. Montessori's approval. Children are excited enough about Christmas and do not need a make believe Father Christmas. They can totally accept that the man they meet is an ordinary man dressed up as Father Christmas. It is just as much fun. But the adults need this fantasy. The adults are depending on the child's *credulity*, that is, her readiness to believe everything she is told. Dr. Montessori often mentions this point. She believed that to take advantage of the credulity was a deep lack of respect for the child. We as adults are satisfying our own needs for fantasy through children, rather than observing and discovering what they really need.

It is also worth noting that Dr. Montessori defended her position on fairy tales in her old age. She said that she wanted to ensure that a great discovery (that of normalization through concentration) would not be lost (Montessori, M., The Child, Society and the World, 1989). She felt that fairy tales were an unnecessary distraction when the child was young. Fairy tales have a place as a part of the culture and as a part of literature. Dr. Montessori challenged the belief that fairy tales were good for small children. Adults and older children, who can differentiate between reality and fantasy, get great value from fairy tales.

9.

A CREATIVE REALITY BASED ENVIRONMENT

Dr. Montessori believed that a reality based environment was necessary for all creative work for the 3-6 year old child.

9.1. Reality as a Basis for Creativity

Practical Life & Reality

Dr. Montessori was quite specific in suggesting practical activities as the means for keeping contact with reality, and ensuring that reality was not boring. She said that practical life activities were the basis of everyone's life and should be presented to the younger child as exciting exercises. When a child learns to pour water his imagination can work on the immediate situation. The child spills the water and adds to his experience, he now knows what it is like to spill water. The next time he is pouring, he can imagine what it would be like to spill water. His imagination and the self control he has learned allow him to move towards making a decision about spilling the water or not.

Practical life exercises help the child to build up skills that provide some of the structures necessary to work creatively.

When a child learns how to use a paintbrush he develops a skill that will allow him to express the fruit of his imagination.

Sensorial Education & Reality

Sensorial exercises provide what Dr. Montessori called an alphabet of impressions for the real world. Practical life activities provided the outer physical structure for imagination, and sensorial exercises provide the mental structure. Dr. Montessori believed that this was the best way to lay a firm foundation for a creative imagination. When a child is aware of what red is and is sensitive to different shades of red, he has a greater power to imagine when he hears about flowers of different reds growing in South America.

"Just as the form of a language is given by its alphabetical sounds and by the rules for arranging its words, so the form of man's mind, the warp into which can be worked all the riches of perception and imagination, is fundamentally a matter of order." (Montessori, M., The Absorbent Mind, Chapter, Through Culture and the Imagination, 1988)

Cultural Subjects & Reality

'Cultural subjects' is a term used to incorporate all cultural aspects of the child's education. In a Montessori school it tends to be used to refer specifically to science, art, music, history and geography. For pre-school children these subjects are based on practical life and sensorial activities. They serve as a firm basis for reality while at the same time introducing wonders of the world.

Children use a sandpaper globe which they feel to help them understand how much land and how much water there is on earth. The imagination now has a concrete base to work on so when the child wants to imagine what it will be like to travel to America for his holidays he has some guides to do this. Children also do some pouring exercises related to land and water forms.

The child pours water into these models and is absorbed in this task. From this he is able to imagine a lake or a bay, with boats and swimmers. Yet these activities are also completely reality based, focussing on what he is actually doing. They provide opportunities for developing concentration.

9.2. The Environment & Language Development

Creative Language Development

The children under 6 years are creative with their language in their everyday activities. They are creative in the way they make words and sentences. They take what they find in the world and turn it into something beautiful and useful. It is their natural inner drive that makes them do that. They absorb the language. There is no painful learning such as we have when we try to learn a second language as adults. Creative language and the skills of language are really the same thing for the child under 6 years and we the adults do not need to do different things to develop language skills and language creativity.

We do not need to force creativity on young children. We do not need to force language on young children. They will use language creatively all the time if we give them the space and remove the obstacles. With language children create words in the most interesting and exciting way as they absorb it and use it in their early interactions with the world.

Preparing the Environment for Language

The task of the adult is to provide an interesting and stimulating environment. The environment must be prepared for language development as with every other part of development. The teacher may read stories, poems and use interesting language in everyday activities. She should remove obstacles, for example she may remove certain games from the room because she sees that they prevent the children from using language in the best way. As the child passes from one stage to another of the sensitive period for language the adult may present interesting activities that appeal to the child. In the first place the child learns to speak well. From there the child will learn to write and read, two of the biggest steps on the road to independent learning.

The Montessori method provides many interesting language activities and the teacher must ensure that they are presented to the children before the sensitive period for language has passed.

Words

Based on the sensitive period for words the Montessori method uses a three period lesson. This is a special method for presenting vocabulary in a precise manner, highlighting the meaning and the pronunciation. In the 3-6 years classroom, many words are presented connected with all the subjects. Children may learn the names of colours, the names of animals in Australia, the names of geometric shapes or the names of leaves in the forest. A Montessori teacher should find many opportunities to present names, using the three period lesson.

When the children can read a little they will have name labels for everything they use. By placing these name labels they increase their vocabulary and refine their reading skills. Teachers need to remember that they do not have to read perfectly to start this process. The pictures, their natural ability to guess and their interest in the topic will help the children. In this way reading remains an exciting activity for the child.

Writing & Reading

Children naturally analyse the sounds in words in this sensitive period. Dr. Montessori decided to develop a method for taking advantage of this in teaching writing and reading. She had discovered that by presenting the sounds of the letters that make up words to the children, they were able to compose and build words. They could write words which they were as yet unable to read. By providing an attractive step-by- step programme the children progressed to reading with ease. The early part of this programme uses all phonetic words but phonograms and non-phonetic words are then presented using the same system.

Two factors are remarkable in the Montessori phonetic reading programme. In the first place writing or word building comes before reading. In the second place, this system must be presented to children at about four years when they are still in the sensitive period for words and how they are composed. This is sensorial reading and writing, not teaching of reading and writing in the traditional manner.

The task of the teacher in this period is to ensure that the children have much practice in use of the movable alphabet. By providing interesting pictures and objects the teacher will ensure that children enjoy this task. It is also useful to allow children to work together on this activity some of the time as they help each other when 'blocks' to progress arise. This activity is best presented before 5 years of age as the children still enjoy the movement and fun without needing to understand everything.

At the same time the teacher needs to provide interesting activities to develop the hand for writing, including tracing letters in the air, in sand and on paper.

Sentence Composition & Grammar

As children progress to being interested in analysing the way in which words make sentences, they will play and experiment with changing words. The Montessori language programme presents children of 5 to 6 years with simple attractive grammar exercises. The children can move words around and discover what happens if adjectives are changed, what happens if word order is changed or even what happens if words are added or left out. Not only are they getting a basis for later grammar, but they are getting opportunities to discover creative ways of using language. These will be attractive exercises for the children because they are in the sensitive period that matches this activity.

To encourage such activities teachers need to remember that children of this age are developing a sense of humour with words. Ensure that the grammar activities are attractive and allow for 'play with words'. The traditional Montessori 'farm' or similar exercises offer great scope for moving words around into amusing combinations. This also gives children a sense of the power of words.

9.3. The Environment & Creative Arts

Freedom & Independence in Practice

When children come into the classroom you must be ready to guarantee their freedom and independence. You must show them how to do everything for themselves. If an exercise is too difficult you must not give it to them or you must show them again. As little helping as possible should be the rule for every Montessori teacher.

Take the child to the shelf and show him where the exercise is. Show him how to clean it afterwards, if necessary, and how to replace it. When you want the child to choose from an array of creative materials you must give great time and energy to showing him how to use it. Otherwise it will not work for him and you will end up having to offer help.

You can make activities more manageable if you plan your environment. Creative arts are possible for children to manage for themselves if you prepare well. Make little name slips for every child. Put them in a place where they can access them. If a child is too young to recognise his name use symbols as well. Then provide glue nearby. In this way he can put his own name on his work. You will have prepared the environment for independent work, the first rule for any Montessori teacher.

Remind yourself that it is an offence to a child's dignity to help. He is able to do it, maybe you are controlling what he does and not allowing him to discover just how much he can do. You must take the focus away from end products. Explain this polity to parents. There will be some end products and more of these as the children get older. Do not make them very important. It is the experience of the work that is important for the child. That is what builds up concentration and good self-esteem, the essentials of character building.

Beauty & Simplicity

Before 6 years the child is absorbing the experiences that inspire his future creativity. He absorbs his culture and develops many of his tastes. You must ensure that he is inspired with good quality things so that his taste in art, music and other creative arts, will be interesting and of quality standard.

The environment must be fitted out with beauty and simplicity in mind. Avoid clutter and fuss. Let the child see what is there and not become over stimulated by too many things, however beautiful and interesting. Place prints of good art at child eye level. Play good music and read good quality language to the children. Take the child out and let him see, hear, smell and touch the beauties of nature. Visits to museums will also provide inspiration for beauty. Inspire the child to a love of beautiful things. This will be the basis for future creativity.

Preparing the Environment for Creative Arts

You should prepare the environment for creative arts just as for any other subject. You must ensure that water is accessible together with a place for emptying water. Then you must place all materials in a place where the children can get them. The best way to prepare for creative arts is to prepare everything needed for one exercise on a tray and to put it on the shelf. You must ensure that each item is usable by a child. There is no point in having anything that needs help from an adult. Paint must be pourable, scissors must be sharp enough and needles must be already threaded or large enough for the children to thread.

When planning the overall environment you need to have a special place in mind for these activities. A special painting corner or easel so that painting can go on each day is required.

You can have a music corner and a special reading corner. By placing these activities carefully you will allow the children to choose these activities when they need to rather than when you think they ought to.

9.4. The Montessori Method & Creative Arts

The Child's Need for Expression

Human beings need to express themselves, be it through language, art, music, drama or some other form. This expression may be seen as a creative act. A person has to create even a sentence before it can be expressed. As adults we realise that we need to express ourselves in a variety of ways and as teachers we acknowledge that it is important to give children the tools of expression and to avoid repressing natural creative expression.

Dr. Montessori believed that the mode of expression varied according to the stage of life one was in. Children under 2 years have to use movement, strong body language, cries, laughs, screams. Between 2 and 6 years they will want to express themselves in language, movement and in everyday activities. Their need to express themselves through creative arts is limited. They prefer to clean a table than paint a picture when they want to express emotion. They prefer to give a hug than to write a poem. Self-expression for the child under 6 years is very concrete and physical. The creative mind is not developed.

The Montessori Approach to Creative Arts

When a child under 6 years is making something it should be treated like any other activity in a Montessori class. Therefore when he is making a collage, he should be able to choose when to make it. The materials to make it should be on the shelf and he should have the freedom to get them when he likes. As the teacher you should demonstrate how to do it and then tell him he can do it whenever he likes. Then he ought to be independent in carrying out the activity. If the child still needs your help after a demonstration then the activity is too difficult.

The common practice in pre-schools is for the teacher to take a group of children and help them to make one art object/product each. Usually the activity requires that the teacher does some of the activity for each child. This does *not* fit in with Montessori principles. It may be necessary to do this on some occasions, such as Christmas when every child is making the same thing. That should be the exception, not the rule. Even at Christmas a good Montessori teacher will plan well and try to avoid large group activities with no free choice.

If you are to uphold the Montessori principles of freedom of choice and of independent activity, you must have a Montessori approach to creative arts. This is a source of much controversy between traditional pre-school teachers and the Montessori method. The issue at stake here is whether the process or the end product is more important. If you are focused on the process rather than the end product you will be able to implement the principles easily, it is the same as for all other Montessori exercises. If you are under pressure from parents to send home little creations each day or even each week, you will find the Montessori approach difficult.

You must examine the very basic Montessori principle, which says that the most important thing you are doing for the child in a Montessori school is building up his concentration and thereby his independent character. You then have to make a decision on following this principle or on producing pretty 'creative' products to send home.

Creative Arts & Holistic Development

Holistic development of the child is central to the Montessori method. Most educational methods nowadays are holistic, but the Montessori method is very particular about applying it in practice. The creative arts are part of this holistic process.

When a child is playing a drum or painting a picture or writing a poem different parts of him are involved. He is working physically and we should pay attention to that when we prepare his skills. He is working emotionally because emotions are a driving force behind creativity. In fact it is the inspiration of the imagination which is driving this creativity and that has an emotional base. The child is also working mentally as he plans his work and again the imagination comes into play. Creative arts are part of holistic education. The challenge for teachers is to ensure that they are taught using Montessori principles.

Developing Skills

The child under 6 years is in a concrete practical phase of life and will be ready to learn practical skills. One of the main ways in which you can support the creative arts in the 3-6 years period is by the teaching of skills. These should be taught as practical life skills. Children can learn how to use clay, how to mix colours, how to keep a workplace clean and how to thread a needle. These exercises are attractive in themselves for a child under 6 while the older child will be anxious to get on with the creative part of the task. Therefore it makes sense to present these skills in the 3-6 years stage. Remember also that by teaching the child to manage his own skills, you are providing him with the key to independent creativity. A child who cannot use a paintbrush neatly will be unable to paint the picture he wants because the water will keep dripping onto his paper.

The manner in which you present these skills in the Montessori school is the same as for any other presentation. They are to be prepared and presented as practical life activities. You should present clearly and then stand back and allow the child freedom to do it himself. Many people interpret this type of presentation as being very controlling and too structured for creative arts. It is important to remember that you are not teaching creativity in these exercises, you are teaching the supporting skills.

"We do not teach drawing by drawing, however, but by providing the opportunity to prepare the instruments of expression. This I consider to be a real aid to free drawing, which [...] encourages the child to continue." (Montessori, M., The Discovery of the Child, Chapter, Drawing and Representative Art, 1966)

Projects

Projects are mainly designed to give children a means to continue learning about something, which has inspired them. They are wonderful tools to create new learning experiences based on a particular aspect of the child's interest. They continue to re-inspire.

Projects also create opportunities to learn social techniques from working in groups and they allow the children to practice their creative arts skills and put them into practical use.

Projects are more common for children over 6 years, but they do have some use for the *older* children in the pre-school. Avoid too many projects for the 3 and 4 year olds. As a pre-school teacher, you must remember that projects should always have a practical life and sensorial basis if they are to be meaningful to the pre-school children.

If the teacher designs the project, which is usually the procedure in pre-school, she will guide the project. You as teacher will be the key to a continuation of inspiration and the stimulus to keep going when activity has reached a boring phase. Projects for pre-school should be short and focussed. Too much information at this age will close their interest down. Dr. Montessori tells of a father who answered his son's question about green leaves with a long explanation on chlorophyll and the sun. "But later he overheard the child muttering to himself, 'All I wanted to know was why leaves were green; not all that stuff about chlorophyll and the sun!'" (Montessori, M., The Absorbent Mind, Chapter, Through Culture.. 1988)

9.5. Dr. Montessori & Drawing

Dr. Montessori had a particular approach to drawing. This approach applies to each age group. In the 3-6 years group she believed drawing was an important part of preparing the hand. She also believed it should be linked to observation and the study of nature and sensorial education. She thought 'free drawing' was not creative because the child had not been given the opportunity to learn the skills to prepare to draw what he wanted to express.

She believed there were two forms of preparation for drawing, both related to other activities in the classroom. Firstly, the child's awareness is heightened and secondly the child's hand is prepared.

The child is made aware of objects and the details in them as he works with nature, parts of plants and other activities that draw attention to details. He notices the veins on a leaf as he studies the parts of a leaf. He has learned to be observant of detail and that is a basis for drawing.

The hand is prepared by many of the practical life and sensorial activities and then the child works with pre-writing activities (such as insets for design). By using this method you are 'preparing' the child for drawing, rather than 'teaching' drawing. Geometric design (insets for design) plays an important part in a Montessori classroom. In the first place children develop an awareness of colour and shape through the sensorial materials. Then they are prepared for drawing by analysing the difficulties in drawing. This is done through geometric design. It is first introduced to pre-school children as a preparation of the hand for writing and for drawing. Dr. Montessori then found that the children loved the design involved, so she introduced the children to intricate patterns. These patterns appealed to the orderly mind of the child, helping with the process of learning about relationships between shapes and lines.

"Thus the individual is perfected by education without intervention in the work already carried out by him spontaneously. In fact, interfering in work done is always an obstacle, which interrupts the inner trend of expression, as happens when direct means are applied to the teaching of drawing. Our way, for drawing as for writing, is called the 'indirect method.'" (Montessori, M., The Discovery of the Child, Chapter, Drawing and Representative Art, 1966)

9.6. Dr. Montessori & Music

Dr. Montessori had a full programme for the teaching of music. There were three elements in this programme.

"Rhythm, harmony, writing and reading are joined together in the end and form three interests, three stories of graded work and joyful experiences, which burst out into the full splendour of one single victory". (Montessori, M. The Discovery of the Child, Chapter, Musical Art, 1966)

She had beautiful and precision-built bells and chime bars for the child to sensorially become aware of tone and pitch. There are also exercises for rhythm. These start with 'Walking on the Line' and work right up to complicated rhythms on note boards. For the child under 6 years Dr. Montessori allowed rhythm to develop naturally.

Finally, she had a series of exercises for the teaching of written music. These boards and notes allow the child to learn to read music using the same kind of attractive activity used in learning to read language. Dr. Montessori believed that music literacy was an element of culture that children ought to be presented with just as language literacy is presented. She therefore wanted us to teach all children to read music. Music performance should not be just for the talented and the artists. Music belongs to us all and should be used as a creative medium. To do this it helps if we are literate in written music. These boards are introduced to children in the pre-school at about the same time as written language is introduced. They are both presented in a sensorial format.

Dr. Montessori lived in an age before hi-fi equipment, in a time when people had to produce their own music to a much greater extent than we do nowadays. Nowadays we listen to tapes of others performing and spontaneous singing is becoming more and more rare. Some teachers believe that it is a loss to children that society does not offer natural music to them as part of their cultural heritage. However, these teachers are not able to teach the children the music because they themselves do not have a musical background. For this reason the Montessori materials for music are perhaps the most neglected in the classroom. Yet they are not so very difficult to use. Teachers should practise with them in a sensorial manner and then they will be able to help the children to do the same.

You are referred to *Dr. Montessori's Own Handbook* (1978) for more on this subject.

9.7.   The Role of the Adult in a Creative Environment

The role of the adult in developing creative arts has many aspects. As a teacher, you may need to do much preparation for creative arts because there is not an array of exciting materials for you to use in this area. You must resort to the Montessori philosophy for guidance. It can be summarised under the following headings:

- Prepare the environment for independence

- Provide an inspiring and beautiful environment

- Present the child with the skills needed

- Demonstrate how to do the activity

- Stand back and allow the freedom for creativity to grow

10.

MONTESSORI PRACTICE IN DAY-CARE

A Montessori centre may be for short sessions or full day-care.

Many Montessori centres are sessional, that is a Montessori class for about three hours for any number of days in the week. The Montessori sessions are run as a means of developing and educating the child. They do not claim to run a childcare service and the babysitting needs of the parents are not taken into account. Then there are also Montessori day-care centres where children stay all day while their parents work. Misunderstandings often arise in cultures where there is a change from sessional to full time day-care. People who are used to Montessori being educational only do not understand how to apply it to general day-care. This is a misunderstanding that can be resolved if the Montessori philosophy is applied fully and carefully in all parts of the day.

10.1. A Whole Philosophy

Montessori teachers sometimes refer to the 'Montessori' part of the day and the 'rest' of the day. This is a serious misunderstanding. They really mean the 'Montessori materials' part of the day. But Montessori is not mainly about the materials. In fact it is not even just a method of education. It is a whole philosophy about life, learning and respect for children's rights.

When we set up a full-time day-care centre, we must not confine Montessori to the working time of the morning and abandon Montessori when the children go outside or 'get tired and need to play'. Inexperienced Montessori teachers often see it this way and interpret Montessori as being pressure on the children to 'learn'. But children are learning all the time. The Montessori method states that they *prefer* to learn from certain kinds of structured activities. It is not only that at they learn better, it is that the child's inner guide wants this structure.

How do we take the principles into the rest of the daily pre-school routines? To a certain extent this is easier in the 0-3 years period because the Montessori method stresses the need to design activities around everyday events. The misunderstanding is more often in 3-6 years groups. Teachers have spent so much time training in the Montessori materials that they forget how much the Montessori principles can be applied to everyday routines, indoor and outdoor. As usual the biggest problem in applying Montessori is to be found in the teacher's attitude because teachers are influenced by so many things besides Montessori. However if the teacher examines his own attitudes he will find it quite possible to apply the Montessori principles and in that way give the children the best opportunities for developing their full personalities.

10.2. Freedom, Independence & Order in Everyday Activities

The same principles will apply to day-care as to any Montessori environment. Freedom, independence and order are still at the top of the list.

For children up to 6 years we can apply principles of order to daily routines from going outside for play to having lunch. Tidying up after lunch can be an orderly routine each day. Parents dropping off and collecting children can be organised so that it follows a steady routine. This helps the child's security. 'Toys', not normally allowed in the prepared environment because they clutter the child's choice, may be brought out in the afternoons. However they should have their own place, their own time and basic Montessori rules about order and respecting others' rights apply at all times. Otherwise children believe that it is up to the mood of the adult and they start to try to manipulate the adult. "Oh please!" they repeat again and again. Many times they say it from habit and not from sincere desire. If they know that there is a time and a place for everything they will accept it. Then they do not waste energy manipulating adults and they can start to enjoy their play/work more.

Freedom of choice need not be limited to choosing when inside the prepared environment. Children should be able to choose about going out or staying in. If a child does not want to go out the adult must ask what is causing the problem and try to solve that, rather than forcing the child to go out. Sometimes all the child needs is a bit of support until she becomes comfortable with the more boisterous activities of the outdoors. When outdoors, children can have choices in what they do. There should also be purposeful activities outdoors, sweeping sand or snow for example.

Independence is the centre of a Montessori curriculum. We must carry this throughout the day. When dressing or undressing in the cloakroom, allow time to show the children what to do and then to stand back and wait while they do it themselves. When tidying up show the children exactly where to put things by doing it yourself the first time. Then allow time for them to do this. Tidying up can be just as exciting as playing. If children do not want to tidy up, the teacher should look to how it is presented. Is it an attractive activity?

There are other principles to apply to day-care. The Montessori teacher should keep it firmly in mind that the principles are there as a whole approach and must be applied to everything. This is not easy and requires initiative, effort and thinking. It also requires a deep understanding of the principles underlying all Montessori activities.

10.3. The Schedule

The schedule is one of the most difficult things for the Montessori teacher to protect. Dr. Montessori believed that children needed a certain length of uninterrupted time working with individual activities each day. This 'work cycle' should be three hours for children over three years. During this period the adult will rarely organise group activities but will allow children to find individual activities that correspond to their personal needs. She believed that the importance of her schools lay in the deep concentration which children build up in such activities.

The more sophisticated the system of education in a culture, the more difficult it is to get this period of uninterrupted concentration. Teachers will be tempted to give the children lessons in everything from a second language to gymnastics to baking. All of these things are important but not at the expense of concentration time. Building up of concentration is at the centre of personality development and social adaptability. When a child has this all other things can be learned with ease. We must not neglect other areas but we must prioritise. Concentration, and therefore a schedule which includes a time for peaceful work and play, is the most important part of the curriculum in the pre-school years.

In practice teachers can make adjustments and at least keep three days per week with an uninterrupted schedule, preferably in the morning. All other activities can be moved to the afternoons. Even maintaining that can be difficult sometimes. The teacher needs to defend the work cycle with strength. The teacher is, after all, the custodian of the environment. That is her job.

10.4. Safety & Hygiene

Safety and hygiene are often enforced at the expense of freedom of movement. How can we get past that stage and give freedom whilst not neglecting safety or hygiene?

Firstly we must be prepared to put some effort into finding creative solutions. Traditionally there was little for us to fall back on but in recent years there are many commercial products coming on the market which incorporate principles of safety and hygiene together with freedom of movement. An example of this is the quality cutlery being produced for small children, *real* knives, forks and spoons which are safe to use.

Hygiene is something all those working with young children must learn about. We must never get careless about infection. It should not stop us from allowing the children to be involved in things such as food preparation. Thorough cleaning routines will protect the child from infection even as she uses the toilet. Involve the child in these routines showing her exactly how to use the toilet and how to wash her hands.

10.5. Health & Nutrition

Dr. Montessori was a medical doctor in the first place and wrote much about the child's healthy development and nutrition. As always, she said that freedom of movement was a key to healthy development. She believed that healthy food and fresh air were also important ingredients in a child's development.

Food is an issue for day-care centres. It is best if the centre controls the food. A member of the staff can be allocated to cook the food. If children bring their own food, parents should be guided on what to provide.

In the first place, food should be nutritious. Fresh and wholesome food must be emphasised. Additives and too much sugar are factors in many foods nowadays so home prepared food and fresh produce are necessary to give children healthy diets.   In the second place, food should be prepared with independence in mind. Food should be in a format that children can manage their own feeding. In the second place courtesy and orderly presentation are central to any Montessori classroom. Therefore children should have well presented and attractive food. They should use table mats, correct cutlery and napkins.

Children will want snacks during the day. Fruit can be cut into suitable pieces.(by the teacher or by the children if they have learned to cut fruit) and left with serving plates and napkins. Drinks (water is the best) can be in very small jugs to pour into an individual glass. Food is not just about physical health. For young children it is one of the focal points of learning to be independent. We must prepare it for both.

10.6. The Curriculum

It is important to have a curriculum for every pre-school. Some educationalists do not understand the need for curriculum for very young children. A curriculum is a plan with underpinning principles. The principle which underpins the Montessori curriculum to the greatest extent is *independence*. You may find that there is a curriculum behind all pre-schools in your country. The curriculum will probably be part of the educational regulations and obligations which you have to follow according to the law for pre-schools and day-care in your country.

A pre-school curriculum as offered by the state may give guidance on the type of activities to offer children, the type of environment, the number of hours to spend on activities, the qualifications of staff and so on. Normally Montessori principles will be able to incorporate these demands. You may have to prove that Montessori does satisfy the criteria of this curriculum. This will involve you looking into the broader Montessori principles to show how they guide all the activities in your centre.

In some cases, the national curriculum may have criteria which are detailed and not close to Montessori principles. You then will have some problems in satisfying the authorities that you are fulfilling your curriculum obligations. You are advised in that instance to explain to the authorities what the Montessori method is about, showing that it is as good as, if not better than, any other method for the child's development.

10.7. Play

Play is seen by most early childhood experts as the chief means of learning and development for all children under 6 years. Play will be a part of any curriculum. The Montessori curriculum includes play in that sense, but the play activities provided will be more structured than many play activities and are not called play. Montessori said it was the child's work.

Constructive play is probably the closest type of play to Montessori's purposeful activities. One of the prime tasks of the Montessori teacher is to show the child how to carry out activities, making them attractive. Then when the child has explored the activity fully himself, she will find deeper value in it.

Social play will happen in a Montessori school just as anywhere else. Children play and co-operate over the sandpit or over the scrubbing of a table. There are times when we need to limit social activities because some children are distracting others who would like to concentrate. The development of concentration is of prime importance because it is the basis of social development. A Montessori teacher should not ask children to stop the social play but should rather restructure the environment, the activities or the routines to limit this type of play if it is interfering with the development of concentration.

However, there is often disagreement about other types of play, such as imaginative play and free play. Dr. Montessori's argument about imaginative play was that the younger children prefer to do the real thing. She stated that two year olds often imitate adults and 'play' imaginative games, such as 'house', 'going to work' and so on. But she claimed that that type of play became less attractive when children learned to carry out real activities, serving real meals, making real cakes, doing real work and other real activities. She was not against imaginative play but believed that there was more to offer children. Role-play is close to imaginative play. Role-play is part of many of the practical life activities in a Montessori environment. In most cases it is also a reality activity and the child is really 'working' or really 'cooking the food for dinner'.

Likewise, free-play is something Dr. Montessori felt was of limited value. She believed it was not wrong but that children preferred and deserved more. At times they need time to be free and just wander. This is allowed in any Montessori school. Free-play is useful but there should be opportunities for many more constructive activities. The child chooses which to use and when.

Toys are often removed from the shelves in a Montessori school because they cause a distraction and confuse clear choice for the children. Dr. Montessori witnessed children turning down toys for her purposeful activities. We do not see that so often in modern society. The children are dazzled by bright well known toys (as advertised on TV for example). This is a form of over-stimulation, a very common problem in wealthy cultures. Toys can be *addictive* and therefore attractive for the wrong reasons. They need to be removed for a time until children have been allowed the privilege of discovering the joy of becoming deeply involved in more focussed tasks such as practical life exercises. The toy can be returned when the child has achieved inner peace. Then the child can choose with more wisdom.

10.8. Staff

Staffing in a day-care centre is obviously an important issue. If staff members do not have Montessori qualifications you may encounter difficulties in enforcing Montessori attitudes. Even trained Montessori teachers with little experience can have difficulty in adopting the right attitude when it comes to freedom. You may find that staff who are trained in another method of pre-school education cause the greatest obstacles to what you are trying to do. They find it difficult to stop 'helping' children according to their training. Untrained staff may be more open to Montessori ideas. However the person's personal attitude will have an impact on this and should be taken into account.

The best policy for staff is to have an ongoing training programme. This should involve at least half of the staff members getting full training in Montessori education. Also provide ongoing weekly or monthly sessions to explain Montessori principles for all the staff.

10.9. Legal Obligations

As a day-care centre you will probably have legal obligations. These may include safety and health, staffing levels, administrative procedures, and curriculum. You must find out what these are and carry them out fully. In some instances, the Montessori procedures may affect the manner in which you carry out these obligations. This would include areas mentioned above such as curriculum, safety, nutrition, hygiene. You are advised to use the Montessori principles as far as possible without transgressing any legal obligations. Then if you find you are limited too much by regulations you can prepare a case to present to the authorities asking them to be more flexible to incorporate Montessori methods. In most cases it is possible to prove that the Montessori method benefits the children. You can use your knowledge of Montessori principles to support your case. In the meantime, abide by the law.

11.

THE ADULT & THE PRE-SCHOOL CHILD

Adults are less involved in the child's life after the age of about 3 years. However between 3 and 6 years of age, they still play a vital and intimate role in his development.

11.1. The Parents' Role

Parents are less involved in the child's pre-school life after the age of about 3 years. The child now has language to communicate his own needs and has also acquired independence in the basic skills of movement, eating, toileting. He has also managed to acquire an understanding of his own independent ego. The ties with the parents are less intense.

However, a pre-school child is actually on a bridge from babyhood to school and the parents have a vital role to play in that. It is not possible to say exactly how much the parent should be involved in the pre-school because this differs for each child. Parents and teachers must see it as the period when the child learns to let go of the deep dependency on his parents. The child needs to know that the parents are not trying to abandon him. The parents need to be interested in what is going on but should not invade the child's space.

Dr. Montessori asked parents to let the child keep his secret. Parents often find it difficult to find the right level in doing this. The first thing is to look to the child. The child always gives the clues. Parents must beware of projecting their own fears onto the children. For example, many parents are lonely when their child goes to pre-school and the child feels this. The child may feel he is abandoning his mother if she keeps saying how much she will miss him. Or if his father tells him every day for a week how excited and proud he is about him starting pre-school, he may feel a huge responsibility to make his father happy. The solution is the same as for many problems in Montessori terms, parents should spend more time observing the child and observing their own attitudes. Then each parent will know what to do in their own particular situation.

11.2. The Teacher's Role

The role of the teacher in pre-school is the same as in all Montessori classrooms. Prepare the environment, present it to the child and then stand back. Many pre-school teachers find this quite difficult to do because the children are 'so small'. But the child is quite well able to teach himself by now.

In modern pre-schools in wealthier societies you will need to face certain parts of your role with great energy and conviction. Keeping simplicity in the prepared environment can be difficult, as parents will want to see an array of elaborate things for their child. Keeping a firm control on 'pure impulse' and disruptive children is more difficult than it was in Dr. Montessori's day because parents expect that you will not restrict their child. For these children it is important that you make a stand and help the child to regain the inner powers, which will allow him to be independent. Remember one of the tasks of the Montessori teacher is to protect the rights of the children and to protect the environment. Therefore it is essential to stop disruptive behaviour. Every Montessori teacher needs to study the role of the Montessori teacher in depth before she will be able to apply any principles.

11.3. Recording & Planning

As a teacher, you should keep records of the pre-school child's activities and the presentations made to that child. It is important to have a record of the presentations made and it is useful to make an extra mark when the child has mastered the exercise. Many experienced teachers manage to keep all this in their heads. However, this has a drawback in that another teacher has no information if she has to take over the group. Records may be kept individually for each child but this may be cumbersome and difficult to maintain. It is quite simple to set up a sheet with the names of the exercises across the top and the names of the children down the left hand side. The page is then divided into little squares, which can be marked for each child for each exercise.

Recording takes time and teachers often neglect it for that reason. It is useful tip to carry a small notebook and pencil in your pocket so that you can make notes throughout the day. Another useful method is to leave the book of records open and in easy reach so that you and other teachers can record after you make each presentation. (Do not let parents see this page as they will be tempted to compare their own child with others.)

Planning for the group is advisable. This should take account of any local regulations on a curriculum for pre-school children. This type of planning includes projects on seasons, on feasts like Christmas, on stories to be read and so on. The planning should leave enough space and be flexible enough to allow for spontaneous projects, which may arise out of an idea which comes from the children.

However planning for what individual children will do does not happen in a Montessori pre-school. The Montessori principles of freedom of choice and spontaneous activity do not allow us to plan what the child will do, only what we will show the child. The child chooses what to do.

The inexperienced teacher may find it useful to have a broad plan (for example - all practical life exercises before November and then sensorial and culture for a few months) to guide him.

But plans can restrict children's spontaneous activity and can restrict the insights gained by teachers during scientific oservation. If you know the Montessori materials well that should be a good enough plan for pre-school children. There can be a place in the recording book for making notes of important things to show the child in the near future. Otherwise planning should be in the form of observation of the child and analysis of the exercises to find the most suitable thing to fill his needs at that time.

It is really important that any planning is only about what the teacher will present. You can never plan what the child will do. He has free choice!

11.4. Parents & Teachers Communicating

Parents and teachers need to communicate about any important events in the child's life. That includes things that the child thinks are important.

It is not wise to have conversations about the child at delivery and collection times. The child of 3 years needs to be included in any conversation. He must not feel he is being spoken about above his head. If there are personal things to be discussed this must be done at a private meeting between you and the parents. These meetings can be arranged regularly but must never be seen as progress reports. Parent meetings are a time of exchanging information about what is going on at school and at home.

Parents should be invited to one or two general group information meetings per year and these should make parents feel involved and informed. Leaflets and notices will also help this.

Educating parents about Montessori is essential. It is not easy to do this, but you can explain about Montessori at meetings, send out little interesting notes and put up interesting quotations. For example, explain why you are willing to wait for twenty minutes for the child to take off his coat and boots.

You may have to make rules about excluding parents, or restricting them, at some points because they interfere too much, in the cloakroom for example. This must always be accompanied by a careful simple explanation about why we do this.

The best way in the world for a parent to learn about the pre-school is to spend an hour observing. You should invite them to do so, making sure that they understand rules of observation beforehand. Parents must not go around helping children. They should only talk to children if invited to and should only praise activities if asked to. These rules apply to their own child too. You must make out a list of these things and then explain why these rules are there.

12.

A Bridge

In the years 3-6, the child is developing much of his personality. He loves to share parts of it with the adults in his life.

Children over 6 years prefer their friends, children under 3 years are not yet able to communicate fully with adults. Therefore 3-6 years is a special time for adults to share in the child's life. However, we must take care that we do not interfere in a very special development that is taking place.

The child is taking the basic skills he has acquired in her first 2.5 or 3 years and refining them so that she is able to go out into the world and use her personality to interact with others. She is finishing off the creation of a personality. Sensitive periods play an important part in this development but there are other faculties at work in the overall development of the child.

Language is being developed and refined, it is even possible to learn to read and write in these years using the sensorial based materials in a Montessori pre-school. At the same time the intellect is creating an orderly structure that allows her to consciously learn more and more in the following years. There are many sensorial activities in a Montessori pre-school that help the child to make this leap. Much of what happens in this phase is done through movement, especially of the hand. The child learns to refine movement so that she can use it for skills that will make her a member of society. A Montessori pre-school will provide a range of practical activities that help this development.

Personality skills such as concentration are learned best in this period. Deviations can be corrected and the child has an opportunity to create internal social skills because her personality has not yet been fixed. Dr. Montessori's views on social development in pre-school are sometimes controversial and require us to study in depth what she meant when she said the ability to concentrate is the basis for social development.

A special characteristic of this age is the move from unconscious to conscious thinking. We can watch as the child crosses one of the biggest bridges of life, making themselves conscious of their world and their own part in it. Consciousness is a major characteristic of being human so the child in those years is becoming aware of being human.

Development of the pre-school child is significant and the corresponding support in a Montessori pre-school requires detailed attention and study in order to provide for the child's needs. A teacher needs to analyse Montessori principles thoroughly when making any decisions about activities in a Montessori prepared environment for children 3-6 years. It is necessary to attend a Montessori practical course to get a clear overview and to understand fully about all activities for this or any other age group.

These early childhood years are being used to refine the basics laid down in the first three years and to prepare to move into a wider world at 6 years of age. There is much more to be done before she is ready to take full part in society but the basic personality is being polished up in the period 3-6 years. This is a bridge from infancy to middle childhood and moving out into the world. When you look at that sweet adorable child in pre-school, never forget how much work she is doing every day.

BIBLIOGRAPHY

Hainstock, E.	Essential Montessori Plume Printing, (Penguin)	1986
Montessori, M	The Montessori Method Schocken Books, New York	1964
Montessori, M	Spontaneous Activity in Education (The Advanced Montessori Method Part 1) Schocken Books, New York	1965
Montessori, M	The Secret of Childhood Ballantine Books, New York	1966
Montessori, M	The Discovery of the Child Kalakshetra Publications, Madras	1966
Montessori, M	To Educate the Human Potential Kalakshetra Publications, Madras	1973
Montessori, M.	Dr. Montessori's Own Handbook Schocken Books, New York	1978
Montessori, M	The Absorbent Mind Clio Press, Oxford	1988
Montessori, M	The Child, Society and the World Clio Press, Oxford ISBN 0-7171-2835-0	1989

Made in the USA
Coppell, TX
07 July 2021

58672060R00074